# I Wrote It, You Read It

# I Wrote It, You Read It

## MARY DIMOND

Copyright © 2013 by Mary Dimond.

Library of Congress Control Number:   2013906375
ISBN:          Hardcover          978-1-4836-2286-6
               Softcover          978-1-4836-2285-9
               Ebook              978-1-4836-2287-3

All rights reserved. No part of this book may be reproduced or transmitted in any form or by any means, electronic or mechanical, including photocopying, recording, or by any information storage and retrieval system, without permission in writing from the copyright owner.

This book was printed in the United States of America.

Rev. date: 04/19/2013

To order additional copies of this book, contact:
Xlibris Corporation
1-888-795-4274
www.Xlibris.com
Orders@Xlibris.com
133914

January 14, 2013

## Dedication

I dedicate my book to Kevin who encouraged me and gave me the *kick in the butt* to get writing. A strong, good looking guy, he was suffering from the wrath of cancer. As a Eucharist Minister at Riverside Hospital, I was privileged to offer him Communion. He inspired me with his love of Jesus and how he longed to be with him in Heaven.

Also I would be amiss if I did not mention my husband, John who has put up with me all 46 years (so far). Much in this book is due to his love and understanding of my faults and failures.

Also to my loving parents who nurtured me, now no doubt watching over me from Heaven. Interestingly, my mother saved every letter I wrote home from the convent so I have much to glean from them, making this as accurate as possible.

Thanks to my neighbor, Sally Pugh, B.S. in Education for proofreading my book.

# Prologue

**Early 1920's**

Dear Santa,
 I've been good. Can you bring me a doll? That is all I want. Thanks, Nannie

---------

**Early Christmas 1930's**
 I am grown up now. I don't need a doll anymore. I need socks and a scarf. Thanks., your friend, Nannie

---------

**Christmas Day, 1944**
 Well I got my doll . . . a real baby! She cries and wets. She has blue eyes and blonde hair. Thank You Jesus for sharing Your birthday with her, her name is
 Mary Elizabeth. Thanks again.

---

**Christmas, 1963**

Jesus, my little girl wants to go far away and stay. She wants to be Your bride! This is a hard thing for me to understand, but I must. Take care of my baby, Mary. As always, Nan

---

**Christmas 1964**

No longer a little girl, all grown up with a new name, Sr. Mary Noel, a pretty name for someone who was born on Christmas day. She's happy now and so am I.

# Chapter 1

Snow was still falling at 6:00 AM on that Christmas morning when a very pregnant mother declared "it's time". An ambulance was summoned as the streets had become almost impassable. Three little boys and a girl were anticipating Santa coming to their house, not having their mommy being hauled out in an ambulance. My brother, Joe Robert, told me that one of the men actually fell, but Mommy was all right. Daddy said they would have to wait for Mommy to come home before they could open their gifts and no sadder faces could be imagined. Later Daddy would take them to Mass, treading the four inches of snow and the little ones stepping into his footprints left by his four buckle Artic boots. Dad's sister arrived later in a taxi to help with the "little ones" and began fixing oatmeal and hot coffee for Dad. The tree was standing in the living room corner decorated with paper chains of red and green paper, pretty bulbs, tinsel, etc., but the gifts were left untouched (although a few probably were shaken).

I was born at 8:30 A.M. It was four days later when Mom brought the baby (me) home. To the delight of the little ones, Joe Robert 11, David John 9, Patricia Lois 7, and James, 1 year old, Mommy came home with a 6 pound little girl! Everyone was happy to open their presents and take turns holding me which wore off pretty soon.

I was baptized Mary Elizabeth on February 18, 1945. My godparents were Mark and Cissy Adelsburger who were neighbors of ours. They never had any children of their own, but loved every child they met. Cissy also played the organ at church for a number of years.

Dad went back to work and my aunt stayed a few days, but Mom was anxious to take her brood under her wing once again. We lived in a two bedroom house with one bathroom and upstairs were bunk beds, and part of it was later partitioned off for an office for Joe, who would go on to college. Eventually the family grew and two more boys were added to our family: Michael and Thomas. My sister, Lois and I eventually shared the front bedroom, and Mom and Dad had the back one. A bathroom schedule was worked out: first come, first got in! Interestingly, my parents never had a car, and we walked or rode the bus everywhere. Mass was a Sunday ritual; we all went to different Masses due to paper routes, etc. Joe and David were altar boys; later on Dad would question the boys about the homily (checking to see if they were really there). They got pretty good at making something up, although not what I heard. My mom was a convert, meaning she was raised Methodist and became Catholic when she married Dad at St. Peter's Church in Columbus on May 1, 1931.

When I went to school at St. Augustine, the nuns were very nice, but stern looking in their habits and coifs. A huge statue of Saint Julie Billiard stood in the hall near the door with the inscription, "HOW GOOD IS THE GOOD GOD". I never forgot those words. "How Good Is The Good God", was frequently heard. One day in school, probably first grade, the teacher asked me my name. I hemmed and hawed awhile but I blurted out "Gloria" as the nun glanced down at her roster. "OK, Gloria, take your seat in row 2". I recall several friends calling me Gloria and I just beamed and got red in the face. I knew this was a tiny "lie", but Mary was just too plain a name for me. I heard the choir sing at Mass, "Gloria in Excelsis Deo," and thought it was just a pretty name. I enjoyed my new identity for a few days, but one evening at supper my father said, "Pass the potatoes, . . . Gloria." I wanted to slip under the table, but three of us shared a loom bench behind the table so I was resigned to the inquisition that took place next. "You were named for the Blessed Mother, the mother of Jesus, since you were born on His birthday and my mother was Elizabeth and your Mother's mother was Mariah a form of Mary, so Mary Elizabeth YOU shall be!" It was never a question, and the next day the sister called me Mary with no input from me, (guess we did have a telephone then)!

I remember my First Holy Communion, and a prayer book with Mary Elizabeth written in it by my father. I guess my fate was sealed at that time.

# Chapter 2

When I was three years old my father took sick. I was too little to know what all was going on then, but we children were shipped out to relatives to care for us. My two brothers, Jim and Mike and I went to southern Ohio with my mother's sister who had older girls to help take care of us. We got to ride on a horse and took baths in the horse's trough! It was summer and there were always fun things to do. Gathering eggs was my favorite. At home we had chores, but here we were on a vacation of sorts.

When we rejoined "the family" several months later, Dad was home in bed and Mom at his bedside a lot. He was very skinny and weak but we were allowed to see him. We learned that Dad was given a drug called Sulfa and was not given enough water with it. It apparently calcified in his kidney and he had to have a kidney removed. It was not certain that Dad would make it, and we were treated by the Charity Newsies to new clothes and presents for that Christmas. Mom would not even consider making funeral arrangements in advance for him, she had faith that he would make it, and prayed to St. Joseph, his patron saint. I remember coming home in the ambulance with him and the driver gave me a "Chicklet" (a square piece of gum—two in a small box).

One day our parish priest, Father Holtzapfel came to visit Dad. While he sat and visited we peeked in the door and tried to hear what was being said. My younger brother, Mike, was known to sneak into the room and get in Father's pocket where he always came out with a piece of candy. None of the rest of us would even attempt such a feat.

I remember too the bedside "sick call set" that was next to Dad's bed. It had candles and holy water and a prayer book. Mom prayed a lot while tending him 24-7 plus taking care of seven children. My brothers and I played Mass with the candles and holy water, even made communion hosts out of bread. We beat bread flat and cut out our make believe hosts with one of Mom's thimbles. Of course we were never allowed to light the candles. Mike and Tom took turns saying our "Mass". I would put a towel over my head and a rosary around my neck as I imitated the nuns from school. Dad did chuckle at our antics.

Dad got better and even returned to work at the railroad. To this day, we all wonder how my parents raised us with such limited funds. We never missed a meal. Mom packed our lunches, even Dad's. We didn't have lunchboxes or even paper bags. Mom wrapped our lunches in newspaper and tied them with a piece of string. As usual, Dad was up and off to work much earlier than us. I was told that one day he picked up what he thought was his lunch, and to his amazement he unwrapped the garbage!! Imagine the laughter at that lunch table. By the time he got home it wasn't so funny, but were told that he always peeked at his lunch after that experience.

We most always had plenty to eat and dessert on Sundays. Potatoes were a mainstay of almost every meal and Mom was a good cook, always trying a "new wrinkle" as she called the latest menu item or dessert. When Dad was seated a prayer was elicited from one of us children before meals. One time my brother began, "I pledge allegiance . . ." and we all laughed, even Mom and Dad.

# Chapter 3

Mom was always home when we got home from school. She wove rag rugs on a loom in the basement. When she sold a few rugs and got paid, she would wrap the money in a handkerchief and tell me to give it to Sr. Anna Francis, our principal, towards our tuition. I wore a blue jumper and white blouse uniform. At times there were four of us in elementary school and Joe, the oldest, was in college. Dave and Jim carried newspapers and my sister Lois babysat. Mom usually had a snack for us after school even if it was graham crackers with butter on them, or part of the pie crust which she made into a tootsie roll with lots of cinnamon and butter. We never had pop or soda then, just milk. If anyone got in trouble at school they were threatened with "you will end up in public school" which, from the way they said it, we thought must be awful.

Dad had a large garden out back and Mom canned a lot of things. We had peach trees and a neighbor had cherry trees which they shared with us. For other things we didn't grow, like TP, meat, etc., mom would take two of us to the store, either walking or on the bus. Mom made her own bread and cakes from scratch.

Even though Mom already had 7 children to feed, her sister in southern Ohio asked if her son Ralph could come live with us while he went to Ohio State; sort of pay back from when my aunt, his mother took care of three of us on the farm when Dad was sick! Dad built bunk beds for the boys upstairs and made room for Ralph and all his books he brought with him. Bricks held up a board and his books lined one wall—boring! On the other hand, my brother Joe was in medical school, and we would sneak upstairs to his "closet room" and look at pictures in his large medical books (nude pic's of men and women) and look at specimens of mice he had preserved in chloroform in baby food jars placed on the 2x4 ledges of his room. I think this is where our sex education began!

We had a large picture in our living room of the Sacred Heart and we would stare at it; it seemed to follow you around wherever you stood in the room. On Palm Sunday, my dad would replace the sheaf of palm behind the picture and burn the old one in our coal fired furnace in the basement. When he would open the door he would say "that's what hell looks like," and that scared me. As a young girl, I was sure I would never do anything that would put me in hell. "I'm going to be a nun!" I blurted out and Dad chuckled. "I thought you wanted to be a dancer", to which I replied, "Yes, a dancing sister."

# Chapter 4

Interestingly, when I graduated from the eighth grade, I was given a small memento and in it was this prayer:

## Your Vocation

My Child,
    God made you
    to know Him
    to love Him
    and to serve Him.
To serve Him in a special work
    is your vocation.
        Perhaps you are to be a priest, or a sister,
        an engineer or a teacher,
        a doctor or a nurse, or something else.
If you do this work for the love of God
    you will be rewarded in Heaven.
        Say this prayer to know your vocation:
Holy Spirit of God, give me light to see what is
the Will of God for me.
    Give me grace
        to do Your Will always.
    Dear Blessed Mother, help me to live and
    die in God's love.
    Guide me in my life's vocation.

                        by: Rev. Henry P. Thiefels, C.S.Sp

My brothers went to an all-boys school, Aquinas High School, run by the Dominican Fathers, and had to wear a tie every school day. Sometimes they wore the same one for a week, and found some of my dad's old ties to be unique. My sister and I went to Sacred Heart, an all-girls school where the Franciscan Sisters taught us business related subjects. My sister was lucky, she only had to go two years to high school at that time. A lot of businessmen would seek Sacred Heart graduates since they knew the type of education we received.

I rode the bus to school and wore uniforms; blue skirts, white blouse, and blue sweater. In the winter, with snow up to my knees, my mom would make me wear boots! Uck! I would carry my tee-strap Capezios to the bus stop and step out of the ugly boots and put the Capezios on and go to school. When I came home, got off the bus, and ah . . . there were my boots right where I left them. "Don't forget your boots," the bus driver would holler as he shut the bus door.

High school was a "breeze" for me and most of the time I ranked number 1 in my class. Oh, there were tricks played, and yes we got caught—sometimes. One time, I opened a can of sardines in class, what was I thinking? I wasn't! Actually it was lunch time and we had to eat in our classroom due to a problem with the stove in the kitchen. I got good grades and my parents were pleased. I excelled at typing and shorthand, so a career in business would suit me quite well.

My junior year I became interested in a volunteer job after hearing one of my classmates, Janet, gave a speech about what she did at a nursing home on Saturdays. After school we talked, and I agreed to meet at a local church where the men from St. Vincent de Paul (a men's Catholic organization) would drive us out to St. Rita's, 1415 East Broad Street. It seemed like a long way out there. I met the Mother Superior, Mother Agnes, and the rest of the sisters ( all five of them) and the other volunteers. We were called Carmelettes since the order of nuns were Carmelites. We wore a yellow pinafore and white blouse. It was mostly a nursing order, but we were not qualified to do more than set the women's hair, cut their fingernails, push the wheelchair-bound to the dining room and help feed them. The day went so fast and I felt so good having been there.

One day, Janet mentioned that the St. Vincent men could not pick us up, but no problem, her brother John drives and would pick us up. Fine with me! He arrived in his '52 Plymouth and Janet said, "Get in, I'm not sitting next to my brother!"

I enjoyed talking to John and asked questions about his car, where he went to school, etc.

On Monday, at school, Janet told me John, was going to ask me for a date. "Fine," I said. He called and we did go to a donkey basketball game which was a fundraiser for a high school where some of his friends attended. There were real donkeys with teachers and coaches riding them! Of course the donkeys had minds of their own and oh so stubborn. They would get close to the basket and the donkey would just sit down. It was a howl! Everyone enjoyed it. I began to see more of John, and continued dating and volunteering at St. Rita's.

About this time my father started showing signs of depression and/or senility. He would not go out, not to church or anywhere. He sat and played solitaire a lot, which must have driven my mom crazy. Mom began working at a bakery and worked nights, so it was necessary that I be home to see to Dad. He would take care of himself, but became extremely withdrawn. Doctors gave him medicine but it didn't seem to have any effect on him.

Well, I began my senior year, became president of the class and volunteered even more at St. Rita's. One day my mother commented, "you spend so much time out there; why don't you just pack up your clothes and move out there?" I was too smug to reply and let her comment just sit with me.

# Chapter 5

We had a new superior at St. Rita's at the time, Mother Immaculate, who could be stern and yet very kind. I saw how she treated the residents; and she began allowing us to do more for them, like bathing, irrigating catheters, writing in the charts, etc. She would not permit "sloppy work" of any kind, but instead of having us do something over, she did it while we watched her "do it the right way." If she wasn't in chapel she was at her big desk with big ledgers. The residents would wander in anytime. She didn't mind, and would summon us to take the resident back to their room after they visited.

We also had parties, sometimes outside when the weather was good. One party was at Halloween and we, along with the residents, dressed up. It was fun! We bobbed for apples and danced; Sr. Lawrence could really dance. We had such a great time as did the residents.

One day, I wandered into Mother's office, not sure why I did. She smiled, closed her ledgers and sat back in her chair. "Well, Mary, I've been wondering how you were getting along?" Somehow I began asking questions about the order of Carmelites, and I even asked, "Are you happy being a nun?" She smiled, and to this day, I remember her response. "You can never be *unhappy in God's House*, doing God's work." I didn't know what to say, "You mean the chapel?" We must have talked for a hour and she just radiated happiness as she talked about the founder of the community, Mother Angeline Teresa, and her dedication to the aged and infirm.

Weeks went by and I was still full of questions. Setting up the dining room one day, Mother asked me to come to her office and get some ledgers after lunch. "Please sit down," she gestured to the large green leather chair nearest her desk. "Am I in trouble?" I blurted out. She chuckled, wanting me to squirm a little. She wore a brown habit with brown scapular and her face was framed with a white face piece and bandeau on her forehead. She had a black veil and rosary beads on her belt. She wore the ugliest black shoes I had ever seen and I asked her, "Are they comfortable?" She gave me some brochures about the Carmelite Sisters for the Aged and Infirm, and I began to have some feelings like "Could I ever wear shoes like that? Am I good enough to be a nun? Could I stand to be in chapel as much as a nun must be?" I loved the thought of wearing the brown habit and taking care of the aged, everywhere, anywhere. She gave me a push one day when she said, "Have you talked to Janet?" Janet, why her? "No, but I will", and left the office heading out to find her. Janet was a quiet and private person, but intense about being a Carmelette and doing a good job, always. She wasn't hard to find, passing out the dinners and pouring coffee. "I need to talk to you," and she just kept pouring the coffee. Not a hint nor smile crossed her face as she must have known what I wanted to know. "Are you . . . . I mean have you talked to Mother Immaculate?" . . . I couldn't stop blubbering. She just looked at me and smiled "Yeah". We both continued serving the dinners before I would catch her heading toward the little chapel. The sisters' long white mantles (cape-like), hung on hooks just outside the door. They wore these mantles only for Mass or services in the chapel. Only the Sanctuary light was on and it was deadly quiet. The sisters' section was neat and tidy with prayer books and other reading material. A statue of St. Teresa of Avila adorned the side altar, wearing the familiar white mantle, brown habit, with a scapular in her hand.

Janet was devout and quiet. I had to know . . . "Are you thinking of entering the convent? this one? answer me!!" She smiled, and she need not say more. We kept it quiet at school, still not sure we would go through with it, or even if they would take us, one or both.

Soon thereafter, I was drying dishes for my mother in the kitchen when I brought up something to her.

"Mom, you know you told me that I spend so much time at St. Rita's and should just pack my clothes and live there?"

"Yeah," . . . and before she could continue . . .

"Well, I am going to do just that!"

"Do what?"

"Enter the convent . . . with Janet". I began to blubber.

"What about John?", she quickly added.

"We have talked about it. He is going into the Navy for two years. I don't know if I will survive it, but at least I want to try."

To this day, I remember Mom looking at me with tears in her eyes and saying, "I've sent two boys to the armed services . . . and now," her voice trailed off as she went to get ready for work. (She worked nights at Riverside Hospital sterilizing equipment so she could be home with Dad during the day.)

# Chapter 6

As president of our class, we began discussing our senior trip. Where to go? About the same time, we learned that one girl, Mary Ann, was going to be entering the Franciscan order, and Patty would enter the Sisters of Charity as Postulants in September. We still had not revealed our plans, Janet nor I.

Our principal was saying "Class, as your senior class trip, I have decided that we would go to Buffalo, New York, Stella the Motherhouse of the Franciscan Sisters". What? I couldn't believe my ears. Did anyone suggest this to her? Where did she get the idea that we would want to do this?

"Mother, with all respect, we need to discuss this further . . ."

"No discussion. Each student will pay $50 and we will take a bus."

I couldn't listen to any more. $50 was a lot of money. Janet and I had begun to work at St. Rita's making minimum wage to get our trousseau together. I just looked at Janet. She just stared straight ahead. She was very troubled by the fact that her mother was having some very serious medical problems, and I am sure she did not want to spend any money on a trip at this time.

"Mother, what if we don't want to go?" . . .

"You can come to school and I will make sure you have plenty of work to do . . . now please sit down".

"We need to discuss this as a class . . ." I countered.

"Miss O'Neil out in the hall," and I gladly marched out there to give her a piece of my mind.

"I am not interested in going to your motherhouse, I will come to school . . . (paused and took a quick breath) . . . I am saving my money to enter the Carmelite community".

"Miss O'Neil you are narrow-minded in your choice of a religious community . . .".

"Excuse me, . . . I will follow my instincts and not to your motherhouse."

With that she ordered me to get my books and leave the school immediately. I went to get my purse and whispered to Janet, "Looks like I just got expelled. How is that going to get me into Carmel . . ."

"Miss O'Neil."

"I'm leaving. I will see the bishop about this."

She told me to not bother him with such nonsense, and she called the housekeeper to tell her not to let me bother the bishop. (note: Auxiliary Bishop Hettinger lived on the premises.)

Well, being expelled was not on my agenda that day and I was really upset. I knew NOT to go home; my mom would be ecstatic thinking this would keep me from entering the religious life. No, I got on the bus and went to St. Rita's, where I met Mother Immaculate right away. She had a strange look on her face when she said, "What are you doing out of school?"

I nearly dissolved in my own body, and tears just spilled over my hot, red cheeks. She was very firm as I followed her to her office. As I began to explain, she handed me the phone and told me to call my mother and tell her where I was. I did that, and was told by my mother that the principal had already called her. "See you later." and I passed the phone back. What next? I told Mother Immaculate what had happened, and she admonished me like a Marine drill sergeant. She told me I would have to apologize on Monday to the class, and apologize to our principal for being rude and discourteous. She cut me no slack, as they say. Then we talked about how this might affect my application for entrance to the Community. She reached into a drawer and handed me an apron and said "Let's do some work, let God handle this; continue to pray about it" and on she went.

I spent the afternoon cleaning wheelchairs, changing linens on half the beds in the house, resetting the dining room for supper, polishing the silver tea set in the Visitor's Parlor, restocking half the infirmary, and serving dinner to the 50 some residents. I was happy to be busy and the other sisters there, Sr. Lawrence and Sister Charles, had to have been "tipped off" as to why I was there. They did not even speak to me! I guess I was being shunned "for the day."

On Monday, I returned to school and was met by the principal before I got to my classroom. I apologized and did just like Mother Immaculate said. Things were just never the same between us after that. And, get this, several more people elected not to go on the trip. Of the sixteen in my class, one was secretly engaged, one was not even Catholic, and one was handicapped . . . and then there were Janet and me. We went to school and they went on their trip. I never even asked if any of them had a good time.

The summer was going fast. Janet and I continued to work at St. Rita's, and one day Mother Immaculate asked us to help her in the laundry room. There, in two black trunks, she had amassed what we needed for our trousseaus, long white flannel nightgowns, long black slips, white handkerchiefs, our Postulant dresses (long black dresses with a cape, white cuffs and collars (made of celluloid), black, brown, and white material for our habits, soap, powder, towels, pen and pencil sets, stationery, etc. WOW! I think we both hugged her, knowing this would make our entrance into Carmel complete. Even prayer books and meditation books were included.

"If you two would like to visit the Motherhouse in New York there is an opportunity for the two of you to go and we will pay for it . . . what do you think?"

"Mother we are knocking ourselves out to get money to enter, and you are doing way too much . . . ."

"That's it, it's final. Get permission from your parents and let me know ASAP," as she ushered us out of the laundry room and upstairs.

Janet and I just looked at each other and laughed.

"They are making this way to easy . . . ." I commented and we went back to setting the dining room up.

"Janet, remember, I'm not a shoe-in . . . I wonder if they will find out about my bad conduct?" Of interest here, although I had excellent grades and ranked number one in the class, I was demoted in rank due to my "conduct" grade.

We both graduated and spent a lot of time with the sisters sewing on name tapes—slips (black), handkerchiefs, underwear, etc. We laughed at the shoes and even were caught trying to walk in them by one of the sisters, who just chuckled. We had very little to buy for our anticipated date of entrance, September 8, 1963. At this time we also found out there were two other girls entering from St. Raphael's Home, also run by the Carmelite Sisters, and we met with them to get acquainted and share our "fears" with them. Ann (later on Sr. David of the Holy Angels,) and Penny (became Sr. Agnes of the Holy Angels).

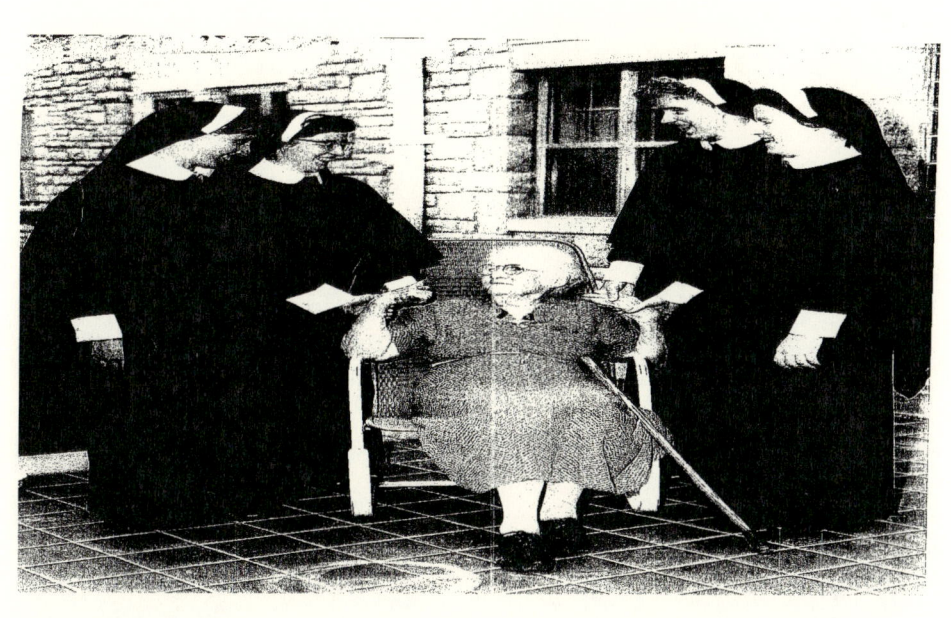

# Chapter 7

Our trip to Avila, the Motherhouse of the Community, in upstate New York was a delight for both of us. We quickly made friends and chatted about everything, most of them were also entering. There was a bulletin board with notes posted regarding everything from request for prayers to private visits with the Mother General, Mother Angeline Teresa, the Foundress of the Community. I was sure she was going to question my "bad conduct" in high school, but she did not. I was too nervous to remember much of what she said. A soft spoken, kind woman, she said we should continue to pray for a vocation and she looked forward to seeing me in September. (Whew!) The day seemed to go so fast, and we attended Benediction in the beautiful Little Flower Chapel before boarding our bus back to the city to catch the train home. Benediction is adoration of the Holy Eucharist enclosed in a monstrance which is elevated during this solemn vigil; special songs and prayers are part of this long time tradition in the Catholic Church.

Summer went even faster at this time. I had a few of my girlfriends over, and they happily cleaned out my closet . . . especially my ten pairs of Capezios in various colors (very popular in early 60's). We had a slumber party, and since we were up all night talking, etc., we went to Mass at 5:30 in the morning. We had all slept in our clothes, no make up, and our hair was less than suitable, but we made our Sunday obligation. Upon leaving the church, the pastor greeted us saying "Are you all going to be nuns?" We just howled all the way to the Donut Shop before we went home and crashed, sleeping all day.

# Chapter 8

Janet's parents were planning a move to Pennsylvania for her dad's job, John was in the Navy and my dad was stable. Mom quit work to be home more with him. My other brother Mike had joined the Navy.

    September 8th finally arrived, and Janet and I met at the airport and said our goodbyes to our families. My niece Cindy seemed rather confused as to where I was going and what for. The flight was less than an hour, and we were about to enter a new phase of our lives . . . tenuously! We took a taxi to 66 Van Cortland Park West, St. Patrick's Home, where we were met by our Postulant Mistress and shown to our dorm rooms where we donned our Postulant dresses. It was the first time we had seen each other in them so we had to get rid of the giggles fast! The shoes were not so bad either, somewhat comfortable. There were 24 Postulants assigned to St. Patrick's and we would find out that there were 24 more Postulants at Mary Manning Walsh Home, another Carmelite Home for the Aged and Infirm, in Brooklyn, across town from where we were.

# Chapter 9

A Postulant is a girl who, for six months, learns the history of the community, what is expected of her in the religious life, and develops a prayer life.

On September 8th we had a ceremony in chapel in which we dedicated ourselves to the Blessed Mother, and received a scapular and prayer book followed by Benediction. It was time to say goodbye to those who had family members there.

We sang my favorite song,

September 8, 1963

> On this day, O beautiful Mother,
> On this day we give thee our love,
> Near thee Madonna, fondly we hover,
> Trusting thy gentle care to prove.
>
> On this day we ask to share
> Dearest Mother thy sweet care
> Aid us ere our feet astray,
> Wander from thy guiding way.
>
> Queen of Angels deign to hear
> Lisping children's humble prayer,
> Your hearts gain, O virgin pure,
> Sweetly to thyself allure.

We were still trying to get used to our long dresses, picking them up when climbing the steps, and the short veils bobby-pinned to our hair; we were afraid they would slip off our head. We then began to learn everyone's names and where they came from. We were to call each other Sister from that day on, I was Sister Mary and Janet was Sr. Janet . . . duh! Some sisters were funny, some pious, but everyone was friendly. We all compared "shoes" and talked about our families.

Our days were filled with Mass, prayers, rosary, employment assignments, serving the residents their meals, and of course eating three meals, and recreation. Recreation was needlework, which some had brought with them, knitting, playing checkers or scrabble, or doing a large puzzle with a few others. We learned that we would have Grand Silence after recreation until after breakfast, so we should get our talking done before bedtime.

Sr. Patricia asked Mother Armand if "letting a little gas go (farts), while getting ready for bed constituted breaking Grand Silence". The look she got could have pierced the Berlin Wall.

Our day began with the ringing of the bell at 6:30 AM. No one dared be late for chapel at 7:15 A.M. because we were supposed to learn the art of "meditation" . . . (snooze time for most of us!). It seemed so pointless in the beginning, most everyone would rather have slept for another half hour. Sr. Patricia would actually snore, and that brought giggles from those who were awake.

The Postulants lived in a dormitory with curtains surrounding our beds, a nightstand, and a locker at the end of the dormitory. All the beds had white bedspreads on them with a small cross lying on the pillow. We pulled the curtains when we left for chapel in the morning. Our days were always full and we learned a lot. At night we had about 15 minutes before our Postulant Mistress would sprinkle holy water on us as we were lying in our beds, "Jesus, Mary and Joseph," lights out, and the next thing we knew, we were awakened by a loud ringing bell. "Deo Gratias" someone was saying. We all figured that was the signal to get up and get dressed . . . in about 15 minutes. Ready for chapel, standing in the foyer in formation (line) and still in Grand Silence. One sister, Sr. Rita, stood near a table and she opened the drawer to find several horn-rimmed and rimless glasses (later we found out they were removed from someone who was laid out in chapel after their funeral). Without so much as a grin, she took the glasses and put them on a statue nearby, left them, and we processed into our places into the chapel. We began every day with Mass and then breakfast, at which time Mother Marie, Superior of St. Patrick's at that time, would lead us in prayer, then announce "Deo Gratias", which meant we could talk quietly while we ate; no longer were we subject to Grand Silence. If she did not say "Deo Gratias" but Benedicte, (Latin for blessings) we were not permitted to talk unless it was absolutely necessary. Of course we could talk to the residents we cared for, but trivial conversation was restricted. In this way we could concentrate on doing God's work, silent and praying.

Sr. Rita was from Boston, and Irish as they come, along with a great sense of humor and compassion for the elderly. She asked a lot of questions too! When she wanted something passed to her she would just say, "Hey toots, pass salt," or whatever. One morning after the oatmeal, sliced oranges and hot rolls, she reached for a banana. Fruit bowls were always fresh on the table all the time. She began to peel the banana and eat it like a monkey. She made the peels flap up and down as she took another bite and finished the banana.

After each meal dishes were washed at the table. It took some getting used to, but it worked beautifully. Two basins, the size of a dinner plate, were stacked with dish towels in between. One pan held soapy water, one rinse water, and one for scraps: peels, bones, etc., were passed before the dish washing began. The routine was, every three sisters were a "team". The middle sister did the washing and then passed the clean plates, etc., to the sister on her left who rinsed and dried. Glasses were always done first. There was little left on plates, as we were told to take as much as we wanted but to eat what we take. The sister on the right collected the dishes and re-set the table all while we were seated. Sisters assigned to the kitchen picked up the basins along with the scrap pan and any food left on the table. All of this took probably 15 minutes before we were dismissed to our Postulant Mistress who gave us instruction on how be a "good sister."

One particular morning, we were awaiting her arrival for class. When she came in she had a banana, a butter knife, and a small saucer which she placed on her desk. Not everyone was privy to the banana-eating antics of Sr. Rita, so they were quite puzzled what the banana was for. Our classes began with a prayer, assignments where we would spend our day learning about caring for the residents, etc. Before the class was over, Sr. Armand proceeded to peel the banana half way and laid it on the saucer where she proceeded to cut it in bite sizes. She glanced up to see if we were "getting" the point. Only Sister Rita could ask "Do you do that with an apple too?" We giggled but were very much aware of the lesson on eating a banana properly.

# Chapter 10

We were permitted to write and receive mail once a week. Packages were always a delight, and we gathered around as they were unwrapped. We shared the mountains of candy and cookies as we wrote our letters home. One Sunday, we were writing home and a very debilitating feeling came over me; I didn't know what to make of it. I didn't have any pain or discomfort other than a heaviness in my heart that would not ease up. Our Postulant Mistress entered the room with another 5# box of chocolates and we politely passed it around.

"Why are you not having any? . . ." someone asked. I thought I would cry! Showing emotions was something we tried to avoid at all cost and we were reminded to "give it up to God", so I just shrugged my shoulders.

Sister Armand said, "Sr. Mary, I think you are homesick . . . it will pass, just pray for strength to get through this phase" and ended with, "Let's all take a break and stroll through Central Park."

One afternoon a flurry of activity took over the convent. "Sister Mary's boyfriend is here" I heard someone say. "What?" I was wilting with the possibility that Sr. Janet's brother, John, was actually here at St. Patrick's; after all he was supposed to be in the Navy, somewhere.

I escaped to the chapel and buried by head in a book. Surely this was an unannounced visit, and he would not be permitted to see Janet, his sister. Well, Mother Marie thought it would be a nice idea for the sisters from Ohio (4 of us) to visit with John and his shipmate, Ray.

Talk about the fox in the hen house, two good-looking guys in Navy dress blues were waiting in the parlor as we entered. Every nerve in

31

my body quivered and I must have turned beet red. I never expected him to see me looking so dowdy as I did that day. After a few awkward moments, we shared news about the past few months. John and his shipmate had been nearby visiting Ray's father in upstate New York. He told us about the ship he was on, the USS Forrestal, which at the time was one of the largest aircraft carriers in the fleet. Our visit was short and the rest of the day I was teased about my "boyfriend," and "oh how good looking he was."

Sometimes a sister would leave very quietly and with no time for goodbyes. The one I remember was very thin, sickly, and wore thick glasses. She seemed to be in the infirmary a lot, crying, and although we showed her compassion, we were not surprised when she did not show up for lunch.

Recreation was a joyous time, although no television, we enjoyed playing scrabble and sometimes had impromptu variety shows. One sister, Sister Joan, who was a Negro, could play almost any musical instrument you put in her hands. She was "awesome" on the drums!

After lunch we usually took a walk outside on the sidewalks of the Bronx, actually Van Cortland Park, a busy but quiet tree-lined street. We were just about a block away, when Sister Armand stopped to see about a woman who had run across the street, waving her hands and wearing a black lacy veil over her face. This was very peculiar and we all watched the two of them converse. It was obvious that Sr. Armand was distressed as she turned to us, all huddled around her, awaiting the revelation that the lady told her.

"President Kennedy has been shot," . . . she choked with emotion as we all turned and headed back to St. Patrick's. Someone started saying the rosary as we picked up the pace to get back and hear the details of the assassination of our first Catholic President. Vice President Lyndon Baines Johnson was sworn in as President. We were glued to the TV or radio wherever we found one on. Everyone was in mourning, the country had lost a giant of a man. We watched his widow shadowing her two children, Caroline and John, as they stood on the steps of the Capitol, and the horse drawn cortege to his final resting place.

Christmas was a beautiful celebration of Jesus' birth, with midnight Mass and singing Christmas hymns. After midnight Mass, we usually had eggnog and cookies before retiring, but this particular evening Sr. Patricia and I approached a dark room . . .

"No one waited up for us I guess," I said, and she replied "I hope they left us some cookies!"

As we flipped on the light, a chorus of "Happy Birthday" began, and I was moved to tears. I didn't recall telling anyone it was my birthday, but Sr. Janet, in her quiet manner, had made it known. Our recreation time sometimes included singing, and I remember one sister, Sister Laura, had a beautiful voice singing soprano like no movie star I had ever heard.

At breakfast one morning, I noticed that Sr. Janet was called out of the refectory (dining hall) and did not return. We finished breakfast and did the dishes as usual before we heard the "ping" of the overheard intercom summoning us to chapel. Taking our places, not knowing what we were going to do, I looked around and did not see Sr. Janet. Sister Armand led us in a prayer, and then announced that Sr. Janet's mother had passed away. She had been ill for several years; colon cancer had taken over her body. Sister Janet would be gone for a few days and we were to keep her family in our prayers, which of course we did. It was a very cold January, and this particular Sunday was "The Feast of the Holy Family".

# Chapter 11

My first assignment for six weeks was the second floor which included men in various stages of life. Average age was probably 80, and some could take care of themselves and some needed total care. Sr. Dennis would supervise and instruct us in the care of these gentlemen. We could give bed baths but understandably we handed them the wash cloth to do their private parts. Sr. Veronica was an LPN and in one instance a man refused to clean himself.

"I just accidentally spilled the cold soapy water on the area . . ." she remarked.

"NO, you didn't!" But no other sister had problems with giving him a bed bath after that.

One of my daily tasks was giving certain men a shave who couldn't do it themselves. I had never done this at St. Rita's, so I was completely in the dark. "Where are the electric razors?" another postulant, Sr. Barbara, asked.

"Here are the safety razors and the shaving cream. Don't waste it, and only use the razor on one man, and afterwards put in it the drawer in his side table," Sr. Dennis advised.

The shaving cream was thick and we lathered up our potential "victims" and began short strokes as we had been instructed by Sr. Dennis. It looked easy when she showed us but after the shaving cream was off, I could see little spots of blood coming from a nick or two. We applied little pieces of paper, and the bleeding was stopped. Of course our gentlemen couldn't see our handiwork, but could feel their faces and thanked us profusely! I wrote home about this and I know my parents were probably worried for the poor men.

As mentioned before, Sr. Veronica gave us classes on nursing. One class in particular was on the heart, the valves, and conditions that occur or precede heart problems. She mentioned 'infarcts', and Sr. Rita could not hold back a giggle. She raised her hand and asked, "How could farts have anything to do with the heart?" We could hardly regain our composure, but Sr. Veronica corrected her and then continued with her class.

"What is one thing you have learned about caring for the aged this week in your own employment?" Sr. Veronica pried us for input to see if we were paying attention.

"Not to breathe when cleaning up puke", Sister Ann spoke up.

"Puke? Is there a better word to use?" she exclaimed and raised her eyebrows in dismay.

"I nearly lost my cookies, too!" she retorted. With that we all snickered, and Sr. Veronica did her best to instruct us in the proper vernacular.

My second assignment was with Sr. Robert in the clinic which I enjoyed very much. She taught us all a class which would help us immensely. While I was in her employment I learned to take blood pressures, pulse readings, treat minor cuts and much more. I also helped her dispense medication and learned the names and what each was for. She was an excellent teacher. I also was in charge of getting patients ready for the dentist and podiatrist visits. They would be brought down from the floors by another Postulant, and I kept moving them in and out as they were treated.

One particular podiatrist was less than patient with our residents and their ingrown toenails, callouses, etc. Usually he would inject a solution in their toe before cutting to numb the area and make it less painful. This day was unlike any other day. He was impatient with the wiggly squirming of a lady, and I noted he did not give her any topical anesthetic ahead of time. She was not one to complain easily and began crying, tears running down her face and soaking into her dress as she grasped the arms of the chair.

"Excuse me, Doctor, but she needs some topical ointment", I blurted out. I tried to console her and patted her shoulder.

"What do you know about this? She does this every time" . . . . the doctor glared at me.

"Oh, please stop him, . . . I can't take this . . ." and with that I said, "STOP". He threw the metal utensil in the basin and it sounded like a bomb went off. He ripped off his plastic protective apron and stormed out the door. I stood in fear of what had just happened.

"Oh, thank you Sister Mary . . . ." was all I heard my patient say as I went looking for Sr. Robert. I didn't have to go far. The doctor was putting on his expensive wool coat and took his hat from the rack as Sr. Robert was listening to his diatribe. I wanted to die! I thought I would!

"I'll be on the next train heading for Ohio" was all I could think about.

Sr. Robert took me aside as I looked at the line of patients who would have been the next victims and shuddered to think what was next.

"We treat our residents, men or women, as we would treat our own parents," began Sr. Robert. "You obviously could feel your patient's pain and did what was necessary. You listened to her, you felt her pain and stopped her from further pain . . ."

"But what about the rest of these residents, will he be back?" I asked.

She smiled and said, "NO." I let out a sigh of relief, "But what about me?"

"You will be just fine. I have had some suspicion about his treatment of the residents for quite sometime," and that is all I heard. I heard the chapel bells ringing, so hanging up my apron, I hurried off to chapel to join the rest of the sisters in prayer. I couldn't tell anyone what had happened until recreation that night.

# Chapter 12

My rotation was finished, and Sr. Robert complimented me for my work and taking the initiative on more than one occasion.

"Don't get anyone else fired!" she laughed, and wandered back to the infirmary.

My next assignment was in the social work office with Sr. Dismas. "What kind of name is Dismas? I wondered, but would never think to ask. She was very intelligent and knew every resident by name. She was always finding things for me to do and time went by fast.

One day she said, "Sister Mary, today we are having a special guest and Mother will meet with her in the parlor. Will you please dust it, bring up the ledgers from 1960 and the cart with the tea cups, . . . . was all I heard her say. I wondered if it was Mother Angeline Teresa coming from the Motherhouse, but I didn't have time to contemplate further who might be visiting us.

An hour later, a hefty woman in her early 70's (probably), wearing a fur piece around her neck that had some type of animal heads on it (I thought it was gross), wearing black boots and very clumsy as she approached our front steps, looking all over the front of the building, and finally ringing the bell. No one was near, so I opened the door and showed her to the brocade chairs in the parlor.

"Would you like some tea?" I asked. She was looking me up and down, sizing me up for who knows what. I was disappointed that our visitor was not Mother Angeline, but none the less I headed to Mother Marie's office for the tea cart.

"Our guest is here, Mother. She is in the parlor."

"Please ask Sister Dismas to join us with the ledgers," she politely stated.

We were seated in the parlor and Miss "animal shoulder-fur" sat very straight and blurted out information demanding what she was rightfully owed. Mother Marie was very kind, opening the large black book and patiently sipping her tea with "Miss Hot Toddy" who seemed increasingly anxious. I still didn't get the picture, standing uncomfortably as the farce played out. Sr. Dismas winked at me as if to say, "we got her number".

"Please accept our condolences on the passing of your brother; he was with us a number of years . . ." and with that Mother was interrupted.

"I know all about that. I was in Chicago and didn't hear of his passing until I saw the notice in the paper. I have come all this way by bus to settle matters and return home . . ." she sounded irritated that Mother was taking her good ole' time, or so it must have seemed to her.

"Sr. Dismas, would you please bring in the house ledger and check book?"

While Sister Dismas went to obtain the items Mother made another attempt to make the woman feel at home. NO she did not want any more tea, and she shifted in the chair, as I noted how strained the legs of the chair must be with her hefty weight.

"As you may not know, your brother was homeless in New York and a policeman walking the beat in Central Park brought him to us. He could not tell us much except he had worked on the railroad. He fit in quite well and loved checkers and never missed a dessert in all his time with us . . ." and she was interrupted by an "Ahem . . . can we just get on with the settlement, please, I have a bus to catch . . . ."

Of course, Mother took out the check book, and from where I stood I could tell it was a rather hefty amount, as she continued with the O's . . . . before she stopped without signing it.

"Sr. Dismas has brought the accounting books for your brother who was a resident here for 4 years before cancer took him. The monthly rate for his room and board shows $1200 a month times 48 months; we can round that off of course."

I was aghast since I had no knowledge of how much it cost to live in these homes with such great care given the residents which I saw on a daily basis, However I did not know this man since he lived here before I entered.

"Mr. Arnold received a new suit every Easter, again I will round that off to $100, times four years and we won't mention his haircuts every week..."

"Now I know he had means and invested money quite often, he was a shrewd man". Our visitor's voice was almost shrill as she drummed her fingers on the desk.

"Well Sr. Dismas has done the homework for us, and as you can see his monthly expenses and burial costs would have exhausted his resources some time ago," as Mother shoved the ledger across the desk for her perusal.

"Well, how was I to know"

"I am sorry you were not informed of his passing, but our attorney had his obituary printed in several cities including Chicago, Des Plains..." again she was interrupted as the lady stood up and flung her fur piece over her shoulder, took another sip of tea and nearly dropped the china cup on the tray.

We watched from the window as she made a hasty retreat.

If this was Social Work, I wasn't sure I wanted to deal with these things. I missed the hands-on treatment of the residents, and most of all the clinic and Sr. Robert.

We became accustomed to seeing death and consoling relatives, bathing the body and waiting until the undertakers arrived. One time we were taking a gentleman from the 5th floor to the ground floor where we had a special "waiting room." We had gotten the gurney and placed the man on it, covered him with two sheets and proceeded to the elevator. (We did not know to use the service elevator which was larger.) When we tried to stand the gurney up so the doors would close, the body gases escaped and Sr. Ann nearly turned white with fright. It was a good thing she was pinned in the corner or I'm afraid Sr. Ann would have taken flight.

"It's OK.... I think...."

# Chapter 13

As our postulant days came to an end, we met the other postulants who were also to join us in the Novitiate which was in upstate New York, Avila on the Hudson. Now we would have more names to learn! . . . and later on we would get our religious names!

    This is probably the best place to talk about the Founder of the Carmelite Sisters for the Aged and Infirm, Mother Angeline Teresa. She was born on January 21, 1893. She was named Brigid and baptized on January 22, 1893, the very day after she was born, in Ireland, the province of Ulster. She was one of five children born to Thomas McCrory and Brigid Taggart McCrory. They later moved to Scotland to seek employment for her father, a steelworker. Brigid Teresa became interested in the Little Sisters of the Poor, entering the Novitiate February 14, 1913. She received the habit and the name Sister M. Angeline September 8, 1913 and Professed March 19, 1915. She came to America October 31, 1915.

    In September 1919 at the early age of 26 she was appointed by the Superiors in France to be a Councilor to assist the Mother Superior in the operation of the Brooklyn Home both in administration and internal community affairs. She made her perpetual vows on April 21, 1925. She was named Mother Superior of Our Lady's Home in the Bronx in September, 1926. Mother Angeline Teresa became a naturalized citizen on April 3, 1933. She and six Little Sisters of the Poor left their community on August 11, 1929. Mother was joined by Sr. M. Louise, Mother M. Leonie, Mother M. Colette of the Blessed

Sacrament, Mother Mary Teresa, Mother M. Alodie, and Mother M. Alexis of Jesus.

The new Community arrived at the very first place of their own, the old rectory of St. Elizabeth's Parish, New York on Sept 3, 1929. This is considered to be the actual foundation date for the Congregation of the Carmelite Sisters for the Aged and Infirm.

As of this date, Mother Angeline has been declared venerable. This took place on Thursday, June 28, 2012. His Holiness, Pope Benedict XVI, authorized the Congregation for the Causes of Saints in Rome to promulgate the decree of Heroic Virtues of their Foundress, Mother Mary Angeline Teresa, O. Carm. (Bridget Teresa McCrory). Venerable Mary Angeline was born in Ireland in 1893 and entered the Little Sisters of the Poor in 1912. While stationed in the Bronx, New York, Venerable Mary Angeline Teresa began a new Congregation for the care of the elderly, the Carmelite Sisters for the Aged and Infirm, in 1929 which is dedicated to giving high quality service to the aged with a special reverence for the sanctity of life. The Sisters conduct seventeen homes for the aged in the United States and one in Ireland. The Motherhouse of the Sisters is in Germantown, New York, Diocese of Albany. While there is no public ceremony associated with becoming Venerable, the faithful are encouraged to pray for their intentions through Venerable Mary Angeline Teresa's intercession.

The above was received from the Motherhouse, in late 2012.

# Chapter 14

The Novitiate is a place where your vocation is really tested, physically and spiritually. The sisters are referred to as Novices, first year or second year (Canonical year). The Motherhouse is on the grounds of upstate New York, along with the Novitiate and Retreat House. This particular year there were 47 of us, moving into the rooms vacated by the Sisters who were being professed; They were ready to take their first vows, so they then moved to the Retreat House to make room for the next group of new Novices (the All Saints Category) A short time later they would be Professed, then they would go to their assignments (obedience's) from Connecticut to Iowa, from Michigan to Florida.

As we unpacked and settled into our assigned rooms, we began discussing what names we would ask for or be given the following day. Each new sister, soon to be Novices (first year) would submit three names on a piece of paper to be considered by the Mother General, Mother Angeline during private audiences with each of us.

"Hey, what name are you asking for?" Sister Patricia asked.

". . . probably Monica Marie (my second grade teacher whom I adored), . . . something with Elizabeth or Mary Noel," I replied.

"There is no Saint Noel, so you probably will get Elizabeth . . ." she responded.

Another sister quickly added, "I'm thinking of my parents names, Norah and Michael", and yet another said, Imagine having my parents names, James and Kathleen," we all nodded in agreement. Janet chimed in with, "I'm hoping to get John Catherine," which again were her parents' names.

One sister exclaimed, "OH MY GOD . . . I am in trouble . . . can you imagine Mildred and Herman?" We all laughed.

We met with Mother Angeline and as expected we gave her our request for a religious name. She wrote on a ledger and smiled as she said, ". . . from this day forward, you will be known as Sister Mary Noel of the Holy Angels." (Our group was known by a category name, the Holy Angels", much like a graduating class is known by the year they graduated.) The previous sisters, senior Novices were the "Teresa's" and they would begin their Canonical year; intense prayer and not leaving the Novitiate grounds except in an emergency.

# Chapter 15

On Easter Monday, 1964, the altar was bedecked with yellow roses and lilies, and tall lit candles. To this day I remember the choir singing, "Let The Holy Anthems Rise," still a favorite of mine.

We received the brown habit of Carmel along with a white veil. This was a big day for us. My mother traveled from Ohio with three of my girlfriends, and Mom said it was the best time she ever had traveling. They were all calling her "Mom" by this time.

We processed into the chapel and knelt at the communion rail. We were all wearing white robes like graduation gowns, along with white high heels. Sometimes wedding dresses are worn, but since there were so many of us we wore the gowns. Our habit, was bound with a white ribbon with our religious name, and handed to us by the Bishop. We were then ushered downstairs to the refectory where another Senior Novice helped us put on the habit, coif and veil for the first time. This was done quickly and in silence as we were about to return to chapel as "Brides of Christ" for the final ceremony before meeting with our families. We just kept looking at each other in awe; how different and beautiful each one looked!

Visiting with our family members took place, and we had a light lunch, toured the grounds and our families caught us up on what was happening at home. My girlfriends were in college and had many stories to tell. Judy wanted to smoke a cigarette and asked where could she go. Mom spoke up and said "no where. You have to stop that bad habit"! Soon it was time to say goodbye. We met in chapel and prayers were said for a safe journey home for our relatives and for the beginning our Novitiate life.

That evening we began to learn each others' names, and what a chore that was! We gathered in the recreation room and heard from our Novice Mistress more of the do and don'ts of being a religious. We were told that we would have "haircuts" in our respective bathrooms and of course in Grand Silence. There were assigned "barbers", some were better than others. Sr. Pius was the best! We had "bunny caps, which were like little white beanies. to wear after that, worn to and from the showers, etc., No one ever shaved their head, which was a misconception we heard from to time. OK, we shaved our underarms, but why bother with our legs, which were shielded in black stockings.

# Chapter 16

We would find our employments posted in the morning after chapel. I do believe we got to sleep in the first day, maybe 7:30 AM, then Mass and breakfast in the refectory.

Our employments could be the kitchen, laundry, Motherhouse, sewing room, typing room, etc. I was assigned the typing room, probably because of my high school business course. I loved Mother Gabriel, who resided at the Motherhouse. (She died in 2012.) She brought me letters to type for Mother Angeline, and other information regarding recruitment or information to send to girls interested in our community. We usually had a morning break. Rolls and doughnuts were plentiful along with juice, coffee and/or tea. Half an hour later we were back to our assigned tasks. Rosary was 11:30, followed by lunch. If this happened to be a silence day, we would have spiritual reading. One Novice would approach the podium where a book awaited her.

One time, Sr. Rita (now Sister Joseph Kathleen) was reading some ancient passages and was not sure of the proper pronunciation so she would just insert whatever came to her mind. ". . . the men had traveled a great distance and finally came to "Poughkeepsie," or "This is the message that came to the prophet Harold in a vision from God", (should have read HABAKKUK) and we nearly choked on our soup (those of us who were listening). I don't think it escaped our Mistress of Novices attention, but nothing was said nor did she read again for awhile.

We followed a rigid schedule from the time we got up until we exhaustedly fell into bed at 9:00 PM. We had classes on religious decorum, our community history, theology, and introduction to nursing, to name a few. We also had time to play baseball, tennis, and take long walks. The whole area was beautiful, not only in autumn; but winter snows were breathtaking.

Unexpectedly my brother, Mike, showed up at the Motherhouse (he had no idea where to find me there). Mother Brendan brought him over to the parlor and summoned me. Wow! How he had changed! He was wearing the white uniform of the Navy, and polite as I never knew him to be—maybe it was the uniform. A lunch was set up for us and all I remember was Mike saying, "Wow, what's all these utensils for?"

Mike was stationed on the USS Willis E. Lee which was in port just off the east coast. As it was late afternoon and he had arrived by taxi, Mother Brendan set him up in the chauffeur's quarters for the night. He left early the next morning, and I was most grateful for the visit.

Later on that day, the sisters assigned to change linens, tidy up the room, etc., brought two boxes of cookies to me.

"Here, I think your brother forgot to bring these to you; he left early you know."

I accepted the boxes but I knew deep down in my heart he did not bring these cookies. One box was delicate tea cookies and the other a mix of Irish soda bread and biscotti. I put them in the break room and we all enjoyed them. Later on I found out Mother Brendan had given them to him!

# Chapter 17

One particular class we had once a week for an hour was theology. A Jesuit priest would come and read out of a book, hardly ever looking up at us, and it was so far over our heads we just tuned him out. Instead, to make it look like we were paying attention and taking notes, we wrote our letters home so that on Sunday we could have more time to recreate, play or just take a nap. Our letters home were to be only one page, front and back, and put on Mother Regina's desk by Sunday evening.

We had been listening to these "religious ramblings" for several weeks, and were busy writing our letters home as usual when all of a sudden, from the back of classroom, one of our sisters stood up and politely told the priest she was "not getting it and had better things to do." With that she walked out of the classroom door. We all sat there numb! He put his head down on the desk, then started picking up his books and papers.

"Do you all feel that way?" he asked. Again we were frozen in our seats. You could have heard the proverbial pin drop. Minutes ticked by. We thought he was about to leave when he said, "OK Sr. Mark, you can come back in." We were stunned. How would he know her name?

A Jekyll and Hyde emerged! He began by telling us to tear up our "letters" and start writing about how do you feel about these classes. Do you share Sr. Mark's feelings? Why can't we do what we want all the time? If something is boring, what can you do to make in interesting? . . . . he just kept throwing out questions. It was hard to keep up with him but everyone was writing. He picked up the first round of our writings and continued prodding us with questions. We were all walking on eggs!

The next week, we ambled into the classroom wondering if there would be more theatrics this week. His format was different. He asked questions, probed us for answers, and we paid close attention. It became clear that this introduction to theology had done a world of good, and we listened intently.

# Chapter 18

These next paragraphs are probably the most horrific and controversial experience in my religious life. At recreation one evening, several sisters commented about hearing someone running down the hallway after lights out, several times. Others, including Sr. John Catherine, had a cell near the elevator and observed that the elevator would go up and down but the doors would not open, nor did anyone get out. This was uncharacteristic since everyone observed Grand Silence. Another incident took place in the chapel, the confessional to be exact. We were told by one of the Jesuit priests who gave us a Day of Recollection, that hearing confessions in a convent was like being "stoned with popcorn," Confession is a cleansing of one's sins or faults, and absolution is given by the priest. As was customary, a purple stole is worn by the priest for this sacrament. One day, the sacristans were frantically looking throughout the chapel for the stole which is usually kept by the priest's side in the confessional. As we entered chapel for confession, we noted the frenzied activity of the sacristans.

"Is this some kind of joke? Who would do such a thing? This is not funny," was whispered about.

". . . here . . . . it is . . . . I think . . . ." was uttered by one of the sacristans. I don't recall where it was found in the chapel, but I saw it was crumpled up in a ball and it looked like papier-mâché. (Later we heard that it was supposedly the devil's semen.) About the same time, a sister had returned to her cell after lunch as usual to wash up and refresh oneself. She noticed that her door was shut, and upon opening it felt a chill as if the window was open. She gasped as she looked at her sink, the cross that normally hung above the sink was facedown, and the enamel on her sink was gone. This caused quite a stir when a plumber was called to replace the sink. He said, "There isn't even enamel in the trap, amazingly clean!"

Sister was moved to another cell since her sink was out of order, and the rumors ran rampant. Another sister found pages of her missal (prayer book) had been "glued" together. Interestingly, several sisters would use unconsecrated hosts (either blemished or cracked, but were not suited for Communion) to make bookmarks, complete with colored golden rays around the host to make it look like it was hovering over a chalice. There were a few other miniscule things that happened, and we began to think this could not positively be done by any one of us.

Late that afternoon, we were summoned to chapel. This was an unusual time for prayers, but we knelt and waited for further instructions. We were instructed by a knock on the pew by Mother Regina to stand, and we followed her out the main door in complete silence. She instructed us to line the drive leading to the chapel and we followed dutifully. After what seemed like a long time, finally a black limousine pulled onto the grounds and wound its way to the Motherhouse.

"Was this the Bishop?" we whispered.

We watched as the lights in the breezeway (connected the Motherhouse to the Chapel) were turned on and proceeded to the Novitiate, both floors, and every room we could see facing us. Some of us began to silently say our rosary. a somber gray cloud hovered over our beloved Avila.

I remember the words of a song that welcomed people to Avila, "Avila is our Home and our Home is Your Home, forever and ever it shall be . . . ." a beautiful song I can hear today.

After that day, nothing more happened. We were quietly informed that a spiritual cleansing had taken place. Was this an exorcism? We were told that the devil would love to get into the Novitiate and win us over, but we triumphed.

# Chapter 19

On a "Day of Recollection", (a day spent in silent prayer and ending with Benediction,) on a beautiful sunny day in autumn several of us sisters would find a secluded spot on the banks of the Hudson River to sit and say our rosary or read. This particular day, we observed a wood-like structure not far from the bank in the water. We had not seen this before but continued watching the boats traverse the water. We prayed as the sun was trying to peek through the nearly bare trees.

Then, a small, flat bottomed boat appeared behind the wood structure and was guided to the bank. Someone noted this and signaled to us to observe the activity at hand. To our horror, this was a man who stepped ashore to relieve himself. We froze and I could feel my heart pounding. At the same time, the chapel bells began to toll, summoning us to Benediction. We couldn't move. Frozen to ground and holding our rosaries and books in our hands, it was too late to make any move. At the sound of the bell the gentleman looked up our way, not sure he could see us, we remained silent and calm. Within a few moments, one of the sisters who knew we were down there began to summon us.

"Sisters, Benediction . . . can you hear me?"

Here we were, white veils flowing in the wispy breeze, frozen to this spot as the gentleman scoured the area. To our amazement, he quickly zipped up and returned to his little boat. We scampered like the squirrels up the hill brushing the leaves off our habits and made post haste to chapel. That night at recreation the sister who called to us when we were witnessing this uncomfortable situation, began to ask us what we were doing. We learned it was a duck blind that obviously was a good hiding spot to aim his shotgun and shoot ducks. We all laughed, bet he didn't get any ducks that day.

One week our Novitiate was hit by a very wicked flu. Hardly anyone was in chapel for Mass, and we didn't find out why until breakfast. Mother announced that several sisters had come down with a case of the virile flu. She reassigned some of us to take care of the ill sisters; one was me. We took broth and tea to their cells, took temps, and put fresh towels in their rooms. This went on for two days before it looked as if the "bug" was letting loose of the Novitiate.

We were at Mass and Sr. John Catherine and I were sacristans. Sacristans set out vestments for Mass, keep the altar linens fresh, and make sure wine and hosts (communion) were plentiful. They also would light the candles on the altar, and in our case that meant three steps up to the high altar with a flame on the end of a holder. We lit the candles, then proceeded back down the steps, backwards. We, of course, had practiced this many times. No, we didn't trip and fall, but knowing Mother Angeline was in her pew, made us a little more cautious.

As I entered our pew, right in front of Mother's, I began to feel lightheaded and a buzzing in my ears. I had never felt this way before. I quickly knelt down and Sr. Janet was looking at me like "What's wrong with you?" is all I remember.

Next thing, I felt someone pull on my shoulders for me to sit down . . .

I felt hot and can not describe the feeling of "passing out" especially in front of the Mother General. Yes, I finally had the flu, and spent a few days in bed. I could proudly proclaim that "Mother Angeline had put her hands on me".

Of importance was our prayer life. Along with the rosary we said the Office, which consisted of prayers said at certain times together in chapel: Matins, Lauds, Compline, and Vespers (Night prayers). If these prayers were not said in chapel, they were to be said quietly alone.

My favorite prayer and song:

## Prayer of Saint Francis Assisi

Lord make me an instrument of your peace!
Where there is hatred . . . let me sow love.
Where there is injury . . . pardon.
Where there is despair . . . hope.
Where there is darkness . . . light,
Where there is sadness . . . joy.

O Divine Master, grant that I may not so much seek
To be consoled . . . as to console,
To be understood . . . . as to understand,
to be loved . . . as to love, for
It is in giving . . . that we receive,
It is in pardoning, that we are pardoned,
It is in dying, that we are born to eternal life.

\* \* \*

# Chapter 21

We had glorious celebrations for feast days, the Feast of St. Theresa, St. Joseph, and of course the holy days of obligation, for instance the Immaculate Conception. For these celebrations we were served special desserts, Baked Alaska, Cherries Jubilee, and they were to die for. We always started our dinner with a "starter", either a glass of juice, half of a grapefruit, etc., but nothing could top having 3 prunes for a breakfast starter. There were a few of us who didn't care for them and found clever ways to get rid of them. Sr. Joseph Kathleen used the sugar bowl one time, and our milk cartons, when empty, could make those little black "yuk" prunes disappear.

Soon it was time for the Senior Novices to profess their vows. Easter Monday was a bright sunny day. A wreath of white roses topped each sisters' veil, and they were radiantly happy. The choir had practiced for weeks for this day. Our choir director was Sr. Adelaide, truly a saint. She had a beautiful voice, played the organ, and directed all the music for Mass, feast days, and special occasions.

Sr. Adelaide had a way of teaching us how to reach the high notes, and had a keen ear for a sour note. One sister tried very hard, but Sr. Adelaide asked her to "lip" it . . . she was proud to be on the top row in the choir loft although she was not permitted to emit a peep! Sister T, if you are reading this you know who you are!!

We were now Senior Novices, and new Junior Novices joined us at Avila. We were instructed to lead by example. Our classes were more directed in Community Life, Theology, and prayer life.

After lunch on Sunday, we wrote letters home then played tennis or took walks (always in threes). I am not sure how it started or who started it, but we made a small grotto in the woods, "Our Lady of the Woods" we called it. We had a small statue and some prayer cards we placed there. As weeks went by more and more things appeared there.

The year continued as we were being primed for our future responsibilities, our prayer life, and taking our first vows of poverty, chastity, and obedience. Our classes explained in depth each of these vows and everyone was anxious for the year to end and to begin life in the missions (one of the fifty-some homes we staffed).

Autumn was upon us and the golden colors filled the acres of Avila. Leaves were floating to the ground, red, yellow, orange, all painted by the Master. We were asked to volunteer to rake leaves from the driveway and we welcomed the chance to be outside. As more and more sisters joined us, "Many hands make light work," was heard more than once. The driveway was long and winding, so it was necessary that delivery trucks could get in with produce and the mail.

We stopped, had hot drinks, cider and donuts, and then went to wash up in our cells. There was a letter on my bed, from my mother. It was unusual that I would get a letter during the week. I quickly washed my hands, sat down on my bed, and opened the letter. Mother Regina would most likely open our mail and sometimes not, but this letter had been opened.

"Dear Mary, I am writing to tell you that your dad is not doing well and is in the hospital. I don't know all the details of what is wrong with him, but he is losing ground every day . . . ."

Mother Regina appeared at my door. "Sister Noel, your mother called the other day and said she wanted me to tell you about your father, and that is when I read the letter. Would you like to take a trip to Ohio to see your father?"

As tears sprang in my eyes, she nodded and said, "I will make arrangements to leave tonight, just rest until I firm things up," and she closed my door quietly.

My head was spinning. How long would it take to get home? Would we get there in time? How is Mom holding up through all of this? I may have drifted off to sleep when Mother shook my shoulder.

"Sr. Noel, shower and change into your good habit. Here is a black veil to wear for the trip. We will leave in an hour". Wow, the black veil is worn by professed sisters and it was an honor to wear it.

Mother Regina accompanied me home. We caught a train and made ourselves comfortable with our rosary and Office (book). It seemed so unreal to see the world whizzing by. People of course stared at us, nodded and were most kind. I told Mother about the time when I was three and my father almost died and he had a kidney removed. He has been ill for quite a few years and Mom has always taken such good care of him. They were married May 1, 1931.

Maybe it was nerves, but I just talked a blue streak. Funny thing, I noticed Mother had kicked off her shoes which was so out of the norm for her.

"Sr. Noel, you can't hear God if you are always talking" was her kind way of telling me to shut up, I am sure of that.

I think we both dozed off and the next thing was the conductor announcing "Columbus, Ohio next stop".

Mother put on her shoes and we gathered our things and alighted from the train. Mother motioned a taxi over to us and I gave the driver my mother's address. Mother looked at her pocket watch and noted it was 6:00 AM.

# Chapter 22

Mom was quite surprised to see us, having coffee and reading the paper as was her usual routine. She fixed us tea and I pointed out pictures on the wall of my brothers, sister, and niece and nephews.

It wasn't long until we arrived at Mt. Carmel Hospital, Mom leading the way. She had been a constant visitor for a week, taking three buses to get there. Walking the gleaming floors and passing familiar statues, St. Joseph, Our Lady of Mount Carmel, etc., we approached Dad's room. Mom rushed right to his side to tell him I was there. Mother Regina was behind me and tugged at my sleeve.

"Sr. Noel, didn't you tell me your father had one kidney?"

"Yes" I responded.

"What do you observe here?" she pointed to my father.

"That my father is in a coma?"

"Think of your nursing classes . . . look at the many bags of saline they are administering . . ."

AH HAH!! It hit me, too much fluid for one kidney. Mother Regina went in search of the head doctor in charge while I tenuously rolled back the dripping IV.

"Mary, you can't do that" Mom said.

"Mom, he can't handle that much fluid with one kidney." Mother Regina went to get the doctor. I spoke to Dad and said a little prayer. He was pale as the pillowcase he lay on, his pulse was thready and his breathing was shallow. There was no outward appearance that he knew me or could even hear me.

"Who did his H&P?" . . . Mother was questioning the doctor as she entered the room. The white coated doctor looked at me, my dad and back to Mother.

"Let me get his chart . . ." and out the door he went.

"I'm going to turn one more off on that side," I said as I stepped to the other side of the bed. Mother nodded and we began to watch Dad's vital signs. The doctor returned moments later and said that Dad had been admitted for dehydration and most likely the beginning of pneumonia. Mom sat down in a chair, and I watched Dad's output (urine from a catheter into his bladder) begin to increase although dark. A nurse came in and checked the IV's and took Dad's temperature but did not say a word to us. This was a Catholic hospital so nuns were not unknown to float around the floors, in fact Mom had given birth to all seven of us here at Mt. Carmel.

What seemed like a long time, perhaps an hour had gone by, when Dad began to stir in his sleep (or comatose state). Mom was again hovering over him and Mother sat by the door saying her Rosary. We wore a five decade rosary on our belt so it was convenient. Dad's pulse became regular and respirations (breathing) were also becoming more regular. I remember Mom turning to me and saying "He squeezed my hand". Whether he did or not, we knew we were turning the corner in his care.

Mother Regina insisted that my mother show her where the cafeteria was, so they meandered off down the hall. I'm sure Mother Regina did this for my mother's sake, to take in some nourishment. Nurses were coming in frequently, making notes and carrying his chart back and forth with them. I sat down in a chair next to Dad's bed, closed my eyes for a minute to say some prayers. I don't know what I said, but I did drift off. To my amazement, Mother didn't seem to notice my siesta when they returned.

Some big changes were taking place, and by late afternoon Dad was sitting up in bed asking for something to eat. He smiled at me, having never seen me in the Carmelite habit.

"Do you know who I am?" I asked him.

He nodded and said, "of course." I introduced him to Mother Regina and a nurse's aid brought in a tray with Jell-O, broth, and tea. He would rather have had coffee but this was a milestone for him to get anything to eat.

Mom said, "Mary, if you had not come to see your dad, he probably would have . . . ." and choked back a tear. She had made all his funeral arrangements; he had received the last rites, and at age 65 he had made his peace with God. But, this however was not his time!

We had a nice luncheon at my brother's house where my niece was completely enthralled with my apparel. My sister-in-law, who is not Catholic, asked Mother Regina, "Don't you get hot in all that . . . ?" (habit) to which Mother just smiled and replied, "I am most comfortable, as I am sure Sr. Noel is . . ."

"I even play tennis and baseball in this habit," I piped in.

The day was nearing time for goodbyes and our return trip was inevitable as there was much to catch up on. As our train pulled away from Columbus and headed east, I thanked Mother for allowing me this special trip.

"Let's pray!" was all she said. She opened her office book and I took the cue to do the same. Somewhere I fell fast asleep and Mother didn't notice, or chose not to see me nod off.

Back at the Novitiate everyone wanted to know how the trip went. They had been praying for my dad and I received several spiritual bouquets. A spiritual bouquet is a list of prayers and things that one does in prayerful request for my intention, in this instance, my dad's return to health. Sometimes they are in the form of a card with beautiful artwork on the cover or just a saying from the Bible. It was very heart-warming to see how much my sisters cared for me in my troublesome days.

# Chapter 23

At the Novitiate things began to get back to normal. Mother allowed me to call home once or twice a week to see how Mom was doing and of course Dad. He was doing fine, ready to be discharged in less than a week. He did not develop pneumonia, but was very weak.

When I said "normal" I meant stressful! I had missed some classes, and although several sisters shared their notes, it wasn't the same. My concentration was poor. My prayer life was not the same, and I was easily distracted. My lackadaisical attitude did not go unnoticed, and Mother summoned me to her office.

"Sister Noel I have noticed that you are somewhat distracted and I understand you are concerned about your family . . . ." she began.

"Mother, I find it hard to concentrate or even enjoy things that I used to enjoy . . ."

"Offer it up to God. Pray for guidance and strength in your vocation," she trailed off.

I don't even know if I listened much. I was having my own "pity party" and nothing seemed the same to me.

"Sister Noel, I would like to see you after recreation," Mother said as she approached me in the hall one day. The day lingered on as my mind was churning things over. Do I have a religious vocation? Can I care for others while ignoring my own parents in their latter years? How do I leave? How do I go about it? Many questions just swirled in my head. I was so preoccupied with my doubts.

That evening recreation seemed to drag on and on. I wasn't in a good mood and it must have been obvious to those near me.

"Are you ill?" and "Did you get bad news from home?" just propelled my way.

I met with Mother and told her I thought it best that I leave. I'm not sure what I said, but she asked me to write a letter to Mother Angeline and ask permission to leave and explain why. It took several weeks but at last I turned it in to Mother Regina who sighed and put it in her desk drawer.

We were at our employment in the chapel, Sr. John Catherine (Janet) and I, cleaning. This was so boring, cleaning things that just were not dirty, let alone dusty. You couldn't tell where you had been. As part of our duties in the chapel, Sr. John Catherine and I would arrange the flowers, carefully weeding out the droopy ones and fluffing up the rest to look half-way decent. One day, we were in the sacristy (the area behind the altar or off to the side in some cases, where the priests would robe for Mass) when one of us took a long-stemmed stephanotis (type of flower) and began a duel! Petals were all over the place as we "duked it out,: Without any warning, one of the Motherhouse sisters, Mother Brendan, entered the sacristy, to our dismay. She brought a box of hosts for us to store in the cabinet, looked about the room and smiled, "Looks like you have been busy." With that she smirked and left quietly the way she came in. Sr. John Catherine and I erupted in quiet laughter and began to clean up!

Sometimes Sr. Luke was sent to the chapel to practice "music" . . . not always the music she was required to do. She was the most talented sister and everyone loved just to sit and listen to her practice. One time she was "practicing" as the All Saints sisters (category behind us were Sister Mary—of All Saints, as we were Sister Mary—of the Holy Angels, began to filter into chapel for the rosary. As we listened from the sacristy, we could not tell what she was playing, a catchy tune no doubt. Finally, she stopped and I made my way to the organ in time to ask her what she was playing.

"Send in the Clowns," she smiled.

# Chapter 24

Feast days were always a big event in and around the chapel. Getting the vestments ready, altar cloths pressed, and of course the flowers. All of this under the ever—watchful eye of Sister Magdalen.

October 3rd is the Feast of St. Theresa, and coincidentally this was a visiting Sunday. Many of the sisters had parents, grandparents, nieces and or nephews coming for the day. Unfortunately, those of us from "way out West" were not so lucky; as it was a long way for one day's visit. We were able to visit with the families as we served lunch, refilled drinks and were kept busy, maybe just ten of us.

The day began with Mass and ended with Benediction. The altar was bedecked with beautiful autumn colored flowers of yellow and orange. Sr. John Catherine and I prepared to light up for Mass. Simultaneously we began to light the first candle when Sr. John Catherine looked my way and whispered, "Johnny is here!" There was not a misstep as we continued in unison to illuminate the altar. I always blushed easily, and this day I felt like I "was on fire."

We set out another set of vestments as Sr. John Catherine's uncle who was a priest, Fr. Arthur Dimond, would concelebrate (offer Mass alongside our chaplain). Her Dad was also in attendance but I could hardly look for them knowing I would dissolve like salt in water!

Mass was beautiful but I doubt I heard much of the homily (sermon) that day. The Junior Novices sat up front and Seniors behind with Mother Regina watching over us. Mother Angeline would come through the breezeway, veil flying in the wind, as she hurried to sit behind us. If anything was wrong she would tap one of us on the shoulder and we would immediately take care of it. She had a keen eye for anything out of place. Only once would you make the same mistake. The cruets (glass holders) were in their place at the right side of the altar, but they were EMPTY. In our haste to set up, we forgot to put the wine in the cruet, but in our defense, we did remember the water!

After Mass, we put out the candles and carried things back to the sacristy where we washed the chalice (gold goblet that holds the wine), put away the vestments and darkened the sacristy.

"Sr. John Catherine, you go ahead and visit with your dad . . . . and John," I said.

"Aren't you coming . . . ." she replied.

"I'll be along, Remember I am serving today . . . ." She smiled and left the chapel.

I knelt before Our Lady and prayed what was my favorite prayer:

"O brilliant star of purity, Mary Immaculate, Our Lady of Lourdes, glorious in your assumption, triumphant in your coronation, show unto us the mercy of the mother of God, Virgin Mary, Queen and Mother, be our comfort, hope, strength and consolation."

It was time to meet and greet, as we would say. I was assigned to serve the trays of sandwiches and pour drinks as needed. There were only about ten of us for this duty so I was glad to keep busy . . . and then, I saw him. He sat between Father Dimond and his dad, also named John. Our eyes met and he lit up like a Christmas tree. Sr. John Catherine took a seat next to them and I was sure I would pour drinks all over the place. How did I get this table? We were assigned front, middle or back of the cafeteria, and to this day I don't know how I handled myself so well. After lunch we gave tours of the grounds, i.e., tennis courts, baseball diamond, sunken garden (private area for meditation, complete with rose bushes and statues of Mary).

Father Dimond, Sr. John Catherine, and her dad walked ahead and John (purposefully) slowly waited for me to join them.

"You look wonderful," John said to me.

"Thanks, so do you".

He began to tell me of his Navy duty and recent trip out to California with his aunt and uncle. He looked great and his smile melted me to the proverbial puddle. A feeling of comfort came over me as we dallied in our walk.

"I have asked permission to leave but I haven't heard when that will be . . ." I blurted out.

"Really? Does Janet know?" he asked.

"No, I don't know when I will tell her, we are not supposed to announce our plans to leave the community to anyone."

"I haven't even told my mom yet, since I don't know how soon I will know for sure" I replied.

"I am going to Columbus and live with grandmother, you remember her, don't you?"

"Oh yes," and he continued.

"I will look for a job there and be in touch with your mom . . ."

With that we heard the bell toll which beckoned us to chapel for Benediction, signaling the end of visiting.

Before I knew what happened, John leaned near me and kissed me on the cheek. (Little did I know, a sister witnessed this from a window.) With that kiss, my departure was sealed. I would talk with Mother Regina tonight and see if Mother Angeline had granted my request to leave.

That evening at recreation, I asked Mother Regina if I could speak to her later.

"Of course," she nodded.

I think she knew what I wanted and I had to wait a bit longer to know my fate. Time went ever so slowly and recreation became mundane for me. I wanted to leave on a positive note. Ever since I had been home to see Dad, I knew Mom had her hands full. She had quit work but there were times when Dad would just up and walk out the door without her knowledge. My brother, Dave, was called to come help her look for him. He sat and played solitaire for hours (One time my brother noted a card on the floor; how could he win?)

Recreation was over, our night prayers were said and I hurried to Mother's office only to find there were five or six ahead of me. As was customary, if you needed something, anything from toothpaste to deodorant, etc., you would ask permission from Mother. discuss needing to see a dentist, doctor, etc. I may have been last, not sure, but when I sat down across from Mother, she knew what I was about to say.

"Have you prayed about your decision?" she inquired.

"Yes, I feel that I couldn't take care of other aged men and women if I can't take care of my own first."

She opened her desk drawer and proceeded to take our my letter, unopened. I nearly gasped!

"Then I will give this to Mother Angeline . . ."

"Thank you, Mother!" I responded with tears in my eyes. How long must I wait now? I became increasingly lax in my prayers and hardly said the rosary any more. The chapel was dreadfully quiet and all I could think about was . . . . John!

# Chapter 25

Unexpectedly one day in early November, Mother came to me in the chapel. My mundane tasks there were getting harder and harder to concentrate on. I had no idea, but she more or less told me to return to my cell after lunch and there I would find my secular clothes (the clothes I entered in . . . 2 1/2 years ago). After I changed into them (hoping they would fit), I was to wait for her. After what seemed an eternity, I was whisked out through the Retreat House to a waiting taxi. (To this day, Janet swears I took her coat, it was November and I probably did, mea culpa.) Surprisingly, there was another girl leaving also. She was in the "All Saints" category. I didn't know Ann very well, she was a junior and from somewhere in Illinois.

It was a very quiet ride to the airport where we boarded what had to be the "smallest" plane I had ever seen. We politely said "goodbye" to Mother and boarded, taking the last two seats. It was with mixed feelings, both happy and sad, frightful and excited, that we headed for New York's LaGuardia. We had only been seated moments when we hit air currents that sent everyone in search of barf bags. Ann and I were up helping the passengers find their "up chuck" bags and telling them to stay calm, take a deep breath, and we would be landing soon.

I was going to my brother's home, Joe Robert, in New Jersey for a "transition" period, so Ann and I parted ways with a hug.

The first thing I wanted to do was get a real haircut, a good fitting bra, and up-to-date clothes. My sister-in-law, Sara, got a babysitter for Joseph and Julie, and we enjoyed a day of shopping. My brother was a lieutenant in the Coast Guard and gone for days at a time. When he did come home to greet me, he didn't say anything about the new me. He always was a tease! My mother made me be his guinea pig for taking the dental exam before he graduated. Lucky for him I cooperated, and he graduated from Ohio State University.

When I got home it was a joyous time! My niece, Cindy, had grown taller and was a sweetheart. Her little brother Davey did not remember me at all, but he was so cute. I babysat them a lot in the years to come.

Mom, of course, was happy I was home. She showed me "my room" complete with a new beautiful bedroom suite with a pink satin comforter.

"John picked it out," she told me. "He even painted the room!" she remarked.

Yes, John was there soon afterwards, eager to show me around Columbus and all the changes that had taken place. I remember the Northland Mall and all the stores there as he drove me around in his '57 Ford. I recall the absolute freedom I felt then.

"Will you marry me?" he asked on February 7th with such a broad smile on his face. He knew my answer as we kissed longingly, the first of many to follow. My family welcomed him into the family.

Our Wedding

Mr. and Mrs. Joseph R. O'Neil, Jr.
request the honour of your presence
at the marriage of their daughter
Mary Elizabeth
to
Mr. John J. Dimond, Jr.
on Saturday, the sixth of August
nineteen hundred and sixty-six
at the eleven a.m. Nuptial High Mass
St. Augustine Catholic Church
Hudson Street and Greenwich

Reception immediately following
Ricardo's Restaurant
1465 Oakland Park

We were married by his uncle, Father Arthur Dimond, on August 6, 1966. My dad would not be able to walk me down the aisle so my brother, Joe Robert, held my arm as we walked to the altar to meet my husband-to-be, John Dimond.

There were the usual "screw ups" . . . like John's tux pants didn't fit, one of the groomsmen didn't show up, and it was hotter than you know where! Kneeling at the altar rail, John would take his arm and swipe his brow, like "wow it's hot," or "when will this be over." I was mortified and gave him one of those "you better quit that" look.

After our reception, we honeymooned in Dallas, Texas. Talk about HOT! John drove his '57 Ford, no air-conditioning, and when he sold it some years later, the imprint of his shirt was still evident on the white interior driver's seat.

# Chapter 26

I began a job at Ohio State University as Secretary to the Chairman, Dr. Taaffe a Catholic man with 10 children. Of course my resume needed some explanation, or so I thought. He didn't bat an eye that I had been a nun, and so I was hired.

One day, a professor stopped to introduce himself to me.

"Where have you worked before coming here to (the Department of ) Geography?" he pried.

I wasn't prepared for an answer and I stammered over the question, turning a brilliant red!

"I was in New York . . ."

"Doing what?"

Now I was stumped. Again, flabbergasted and annoyed at his inquisition . . .

"Ah hah! Woman of ill repute in the red light district of New York."

"Please, I have work to do," and I snubbed him royally. Later it bothered me to the point I sought the advice of the Chairman, Mr. Taaffe. I explained how I felt and what he said, etc.

"I will see that he does not EVER bother you again," he remarked.

It could have been the next day that a very humbled, red-faced, (not enough expletives to mention here) peeked in the office and with a soft apologetic voice said, "I'm sorry" and hurried away. Later that week he left a small, beautiful wood-inlaid box on my desk with a tiny "so very sorry" note. The rest of the time went quite well. I actually developed a class card system that worked so well I was summoned to the Main Library to explain it to other departments. To me it was just a matter of convenience. I would get a class roster from each professor and give him or her only those cards. Most of the ones I kept were students who had dropped the course anyway. The professors were very lax, not checking the student rosters for anyone not in their class.

Our first Christmas was wonderful, and we decided to attend midnight Mass at Mount Carmel Hospital where Fr. Dimond was assigned. I loved the Christmas Mass, songs, poinsettias, manger figures, and the intimacy that John and I shared.

January was cold, probably the coldest I had experience in quite awhile. John was up and gone to work when my alarm went off. Oh, no . . . . I felt terrible and hugged the commode for most of the morning. In the afternoon I felt great and had a cleaning attack, polishing and shining everything in our tiny apartment. John of course assumed I had gone to work so he came home bringing take-out Chinese for dinner. The smell of it sent me racing to the bathroom.

"I must have the flu," I told him. "I hope I can go to work tomorrow," but as luck would have it, again I felt terrible in the morning.

I called my mother around noon to see how Dad was doing since I was feeling better now.

After I told her how I had missed two days of work, she quizzed me, "Are you pregnant?"

Ah, hah!! Being Catholic and not using any contraceptive it had not crossed my mind,(what was I thinking?) but it all fit: morning sickness. Of course, Mom was happy for us, and John too, although overwhelmed with the responsibility of a "little one."

I was blissfully happy, gathering things I would need and of course working as much as I could. I was very healthy and the chances of delivering a healthy baby were very high. I had not gained a lot of weight, and working made the time go fast.

John's aunt, Aunt Marg, came down from Toledo and stayed with us hoping to help me with the baby. Early on October 11, 1967 John and I became parents to Catherine Marie, 6 pounds 10 ounces, a very good baby. She was beautiful, and John began to learn how to change a diaper. He was a very dedicated Dad and helped as much as he could. Since I was breastfeeding, he couldn't help much with the feedings, and life continued as usual.

Sr. John Catherine was able to come home for Cathy's baptism. She looked wonderful and seemed happy at Carmel Hall in Detroit.

# Chapter 27

After nine months of doing this "mommy thing" I needed a break. John's Aunt Marg volunteered to take care of Cathy and they (Aunt Marg and Uncle Bob) offered us the use of their boat and even the trailer to stay in just north of Toledo, in Michigan. John loved to fish and I was just getting the hang of it, when . . . it began to rain. We thought of Noah and his Ark. We could use one. After three or four days of rain and being isolated, I missed our daughter, and we decided to return to Toledo, get her and return home.

It wasn't much longer and the proverbial light bulb went on . . . . I was pregnant! Again, John worried about financially having another baby, but I told him God would provide. "What, diapers?" . . . since we would soon have two to diaper and feed.

March 27, 1969 our second daughter was born after a long day. Aunt Marg was here to take care of Cathy and my mom came to Mount Carmel to see her newest grandchild. John was proud, and we decided to name her Margaret Sue. "(His mother was Catherine and her sister was Margaret or in this case, Aunt Marg)."

After everyone left the hospital I had been sleeping very sound. I became aware of a commotion in the room and lifted my head to see a nurse, a priest, and a little tiny nun, Sister Rose Thomas, CSG, bringing an isolate into the room with my baby enclosed.

"What is your baby's baptismal name?" the priest inquired.

"Wait, my husband just left. We were going to have Father Dimond . . . ." I began.

"We don't have time . . ." responded the priest.

The little nun, Sr. Rose spoke softly to me. "They are sending your daughter to Children's Hospital for further care. It is imperative we baptize her before she goes . . ."

"OK, fine. Margaret Sue"

"I baptize thee Margaret Sue . . ." the priest began and soon they were whisking her away. I called home, but by mistake I called my mother (our phone numbers were similar).

"Mary, you must be mistaken. We just left there and everything was fine" Mom said.

"They told me to have John go to Children's and have her admitted, that is as much as I know . . . please call John for me," and I drifted back to sleep.

The next day, my obstetrician waltzed into my room early.

"How's the beautiful little girl doing?" he inquired.

"You don't know? They took her to Children's last night . . ." and he was out the door saying he would be back.

Later he would tell me that the pediatrician would be in to explain they suspected Margaret had Hyaline' Membrane Disease. That was Greek to me, what the hell did that mean? (The Kennedy's had a baby boy, Patrick Bouvier Kennedy, who died of the same ailment August '63). I couldn't sleep, and the doctor ordered a sedative for me so I could rest.

As soon as I was discharged, John and I headed for Children's Hospital. We strenuously washed our hands up to our elbows, gowned up before entering the area; and stood in an ultraviolet light before they allowed us to get close to her. Seeing my baby in an incubator with needles in her scalp, tiny intravenous lines providing medication, this tiny 5 pound infant with brown hair was lying limp. Oxygen was being pumped into the enclosed chamber and her chest heaved with every breath she tried to take.

The doctors told us that every day was another step forward and it would take some time for her to regain full capacity in her lungs. John returned to work but I somehow managed to get to Children's every day. My sister-in-law, Peggy, would take me, and Aunt Marg was still helping out with Cathy. This baby would be her namesake and she was thrilled.

It happened to be Holy Thursday and Peggy came to take me to the hospital. I kissed Cathy bye-bye and told Aunt Marg we wouldn't be long. I was beginning to wear down, not sleeping well and trying to keep all the "balls in the air."

As we approached the sinks to start scrubbing up a doctor whom I had seen in the days before greeted us.

"How is Margaret doing?" I inquired.

I was not prepared for his reply, his curt remark and lack of medical courtesy.

"Do you realize that the only thing keeping your child alive are those tubes that are plugged in . . ."

I thought I would scream for him to stop. I couldn't hear any more of his diatribe. I abruptly stopped scrubbing up, turned to him and said, "You better not pull the plug! It is God's decision . . ." and with tears in my eyes, I pushed my way into the room to glance once again at the tiny, apparently lifeless body. I never held her, let alone touched her tiny fingers.

For once in my life, I felt helpless, hopeless, and so torn. John and I had talked every night and he was concerned about the financial bills we were incurring. It seemed every specialist in the city was sending us an EOMB (Explanation of Medical Benefits) after the insurance had paid their part. John would say he was thinking with his head and I was thinking with my heart, and he was so correct!

I readily remembered that this was Holy Thursday and I attended services that evening holding John's hand for support. I prayed like never before, I called on St. Ann (patron saint of mothers) and St. Teresa to see me through this and bring my baby home "if it be the Will of God."

John had Friday off. We did some shopping and took Cathy to the park just to get out of the house. Aunt Marg would have to leave soon, and she made up some delicious meals and froze them for us for later.

Good Friday is usually an austere and somber day, recalling that 3:00 PM was supposedly the time when Jesus died on the cross for us.

Services were, as predicted, austere and somber with the altar being stripped, and the Blessed Sacrament was exposed on the altar and would be all night, until services at noon on Saturday.

"Lord, Jesus, You have my baby in Your hands. If it be your will and you want her back in Heaven, then let her passing take place while You are on the altar . . ." I prayed and cried at the same time.

# Chapter 28

Saturday was a sunny day. John was out in the yard with Cathy as I boiled eggs for them to color later on, when Peggy would take me to the hospital. I looked at the clock and thought I better fix lunch for us, when the phone rang. My heart stopped. I grabbed for it like it would disappear if I didn't get it.

"Mrs. Dimond, this is the doctor on call at Children's . . . ." he began.

"Yes, what is it?"

"Can you and your husband come here as soon as possible?"

"Of course," and I hung up and hollered for John to come in. I told him we needed to go to the hospital quickly.

As he washed up, I fed Cathy and called a nearby girl who could baby sit. Minutes flew by and we arrived at the hospital. I was half running down the hallway and felt that John was just "lagging" behind.

"Hi, you must be Mr. and Mrs. Dimond, Margaret Sue's parents" a doctor in green scrubs began.

"Has her condition worsened?" I stammered.

"Actually, Mrs. Dimond, she died at 11:30, just a half hour ago . . .". He began discussing with John the need for an autopsy and I lost it.

"We came here so you could get our permission to do an autopsy?" John hushed me up as he continued talking with the doctor. The unit Margaret had been in was dark, and I couldn't wait to get out of there. John and I hugged for what seemed like an hour.

"What's next?" I asked as we drove home.

"The doctor said to call back and let them know what funeral home would be picking her up . . . ."

A flood of never ending tears and sheer exhaustion took over my body. My sister-in-law, called to see what time I wanted to go to the hospital, and she quickly surmised that it would not be necessary.

John went to a local funeral home, Kelly's Funeral Home on High Street, and made arrangements while I put Cathy down for a nap. He was back and tried to assuage me with hugs. I couldn't or wouldn't talk. God had taken my baby from me; nine months wasted and now nothing to show for my labor.

Peggy showed up and we apprised her of the situation.

"What a beautiful day to go to Heaven," I remarked as the sun shone brightly; it was nearly 3:30 PM.

John said Mr. Kelly would arrange for her burial and we could have a viewing on Sunday evening, due to this Sunday being Easter Sunday, and burial on Monday. I hurriedly went through some clothes I had for Cathy, her baptismal gown which I had planned to use for Margaret's baptism; now I would bury her in it. Peggy offered to take them to Kelly's for us. I was numb and even Cathy's little antics brought no comfort to me. John was on the telephone to Aunt Marg, my mother, his father and sister, and I was like a robot. I couldn't pray. I thought Jesus had abandoned me.

"How could this happen to me? Was this my due justice for leaving the convent?" My heart was broken! "Would I ever have another child?"

Father Dimond came to visit that day and plan a funeral for us. I was hardly up for company but his calm demeanor and kindness was enough to soften my heart and allow me a quiet, if not reverent, attitude. We agreed to viewing at the funeral home for an hour, and services at the graveside on Monday. Funeral Masses were not necessary since the baby would have gone to heaven immediately, Father explained. Father was always so accommodating, and I felt better knowing some sort of religious services would be held.

Sunday evening we met and greeted our family and friends, putting on our best "we're fine" faces. I remember the mother-in-law of my best friend from high school talking about her kindergarten class and how the gerbils seemed to multiply. 5 times every day. Why do people talk about such mundane, boring and stupid things while my baby lies in a closed coffin?

Our babysitter had school on Monday so her, mother was kind enough to come and watch Cathy. Again, strange miniscule details are ever indelibly in my recollections, but I know for a fact that the money we paid her, she left on our television and I saw it later.

My heart began to heal as we pulled into St. Joseph's Cemetery. This was perfect, as St. Joseph was an honored Saint, the father of baby Jesus. The small procession of cars would wind their way toward the back, passing sections named St. John, St. Peter and Assumption. The cars slowed and stopped. As we alighted from our cars, I noticed a sign noting the section where she was to be buried; "Guardian Angels." This was an area of the cemetery dedicated for babies only. How perfect! I looked skyward and whispered, "Thy Will Be Done.".

My brothers, Jim and Tom, bought a beautiful marker, complete with an angel on it. Our lives began to get back to normal. Soon after, I asked John, "How could we afford such a beautiful ceremony? We are getting bills from the hospital and we can pay them on a sliding scale. What about Mr. Kelly?"

"I think he knew the situation; he charged us $100 . . ." he spoke just above a whisper.

# Chapter 29

John went back to work and I was fortunate to be able to stay home and take care of Cathy. My motherly instincts took over from time to time and I wanted another baby, boy or girl, it didn't matter, just another child. Our finances had not changed. As a matter of fact, the day I sat and wrote the final check to Children's Hospital some seven months later, my prayers were answered. I fixed a "special" dinner although nothing fancy, and greeted my husband when he came in from work, "Honey, I think I'm pregnant!"

Our son, John Joseph III, was born on June 17, 1970. The nurse handed him to my husband, saying, "Happy Father's Day!"

Cathy was enthralled with her little brother and kept a watchful eye on him. One time I was in the kitchen and when I returned to the living room where I had laid Johnny on the couch, Cathy had picked him up and put him on the gold rocking chair.

Once, John (husband) was watching the two children while I was grocery shopping. As it happened, he had to change Johnny's diaper and that was no easy task, even for me at times. When I returned, all seemed well and I breathed a sigh of relief until I went to change Johnny's diaper later that afternoon. Years later we would recall that Daddy had used masking tape on Johnny's diaper to keep it on him.

"I was afraid I would stick him!" and that, my friends, was the first PAMPERS.

# Chapter 30

Life was good. Cathy was the quiet child and John just the opposite. I became involved in PTA and Girl Scouts. One of the best experiences I ever had was being the Director of Day Camp at Sugarbush Day Camp. I directed about 12 leaders, including my sister, Lois, in activities, and led many a hike. One particular Girl Scout came wearing white shorts and a yellow gingham blouse, the day we were going to explore the banks of a small stream for red clay to mold it into little baskets, turtles, etc., and fire them over our camp fire. At first she wanted nothing to do with the activity but before long she was right in there, splashing and clawing for clay, smiling the whole time. The next day she wore dark pants and a tan colored blouse, ready to explore and create. One of the girls brought something to me I had never seen, but it was an interesting piece. It looked like a small canon ball, about the size of a tennis ball. It was black as coal, heavier than a usual rock this size, and just intrigued me.

Since I had been employed in the geography department at OSU, I knew a few professors and took the specimen to one of them. His eyes lit up when he saw what I had in my hand.

"That is a concretion!" he smiled as he turned it over and over in his hands. "Where did you find this?", and I went on to explain where and how we found it. It is a rare piece and for a time it was showcased in the Ranger Station for all to see.

Since no one else in the city would take the responsibility of being the Director, all Scouts were pooled into one camp, mine! We had a number of girls who unfortunately did not always have a lunch. Others would share with them, so we decided to have more "campfire lunches", sometimes a potato, carrots and an onion cooked right on the coals in aluminum foil.

Somehow I was talked into letting them put my hair in "corn rows" and talk about torture! As the day wore on the braiding got tighter and tighter like a vise around my head.

Another memorable time, a tornado siren wailed, and of course we were not prepared for that. A park ranger came by and instructed us to get the girls inside a cement shelter which was used to store lawnmowers and the like. First we had to get those machines out of the garage. One leader, Melvina, had been raised on a farm and she was quite a mover and shaker. By the time it was emptied, clouds were getting very dark and a breeze was picking up dust and dirt. We got the girls inside this 12 x 12 shelter and everyone looked at me, what now?

"OK, we will make the best of it," I said. I prayed about every prayer I could remember between getting grilled on what we were going to do.

"Now, for the next hour we will have a talent show. You have only minutes to decide what you will do . . . ."

"I can sing," someone clamored. "Can I go first?" and she was ushered onto an overturned box and began her rendition of "God Bless America." We all joined in and my nerves began to quiet. Talent like I had never noticed, enthralled all 90 of the scouts and leaders. Some told jokes, recited a poem, tap danced or maybe it was ballet, with no music, but we had a grand ole' time. The ranger came by and said it was an all clear, and some parents came to pick up their daughters. We suffered little effects from the wind, and boarded our busses home.

Girl Scouts are known for their cookie sales, and everyone knows the thin mint, chocolate chips, etc., and our troop really put an effort into their sales. I was to have over 600 boxes of cookies delivered to my home on March 16, 1979. We had moved furniture out of the dining room to make room for the cargo, and I made signs where to put the different varieties. The phone rang just as I finished putting the signs up.

"Hello," I said. It was my mother and I could tell by her whispered plea and her voice, she needed help.

# Chapter 31

John came in from work and John and Cathy were doing homework. "Mom called, I need to go over and see what's going on," I told him as I grabbed a sweater and told him what to fix for dinner. It was a gloomy night and seemed there were more cars on the road than normal.

When I arrived, Mom stepped out on the porch and talked in hushed tones.

"Your dad has been in bed most of the day, and will not eat. He had coffee in bed, but something is bothering him. I heard him in the bathroom last night, maybe a thud or something; but he was able to get back in bed" . . . . she turned and opened the door and we went inside.

I didn't hesitate, went in to Dad's room and turned on the light. Dad was lying in a fetal position with his eyes closed. I knelt down next to the bed and asked my father if he was hurt.

No answer, so I asked again, louder this time.

"Dad, you can't just lie here this long and Mom said you have not eaten anything, can you open your eyes for me?" It seemed like 10 minutes before he opened his eyes and said, "Turn off the light!" That was my dad, one light on in the house at a time!

I was able to get him on his back, and realized he was in pain.

"Dad, when you fell in the bathroom last night, what side did you fall on?" He was surprised that I knew this, but patted his right side, his hip. His right leg was drawn up more than the left and he was certainly guarding it.

Mom decided to get him into some dry clothes while I went to call the doctor. He wanted to see Dad as soon as we took him there. We called my sister-in-law, Peggy, who would drop her children off to Lois, my sister, and be over as soon as possible.

An x-ray revealed a slight crack in Dad's pelvis and he prescribed some pain pills. The doctor said it would "knit" itself, but it would take time and rest in bed.

Mom continued to cook Dad's favorite meals, and this day was St. Patrick's Day. Mom had planned corned beef and cabbage and it smelled so good when I walked in later that evening. I hadn't been home from work, so Mom invited me to sit down and eat with her. "He hardly eats anything . . . doesn't even want a beer. What am I going to do?"

Mom had gotten a hospital bed, and the men who brought it set it up in the kitchen "addition" Mom had had built years before. Most of the family had come to see Dad, bringing food for Mom who would send it home with me "for my kids". It was Saturday night, Mom had the TV on watching "The Lawrence Welk Show" which was of course a tribute to the Irish, "My Wild Irish Eyes" was sung among Dad's other favorites. Mom was trying to interest him to eat a spoonful of tapioca, but it was useless.

"Mother, get these kids something to eat . . . ." was about all he would say. He was reverting back to when we were just little tykes.

He began to run a temp and sleep 50 minutes of every hour. I decided to call Father Dimond who would give Dad the last rites of the church (now referred to as the Sacrament of the Sick). He promised to come and I made a few more calls to Dave, Tom, and Jim. Jim lived in Indianapolis and said he would be coming over, probably tomorrow.

Father Dimond came and said the usual prayers, and offered Dad Communion, but Dad wouldn't even open his cracked, dry lips.

"Dad, this is Jesus" . . . I turned to Father and asked if I could try a tiny piece of the host. He nodded and I broke a tiny piece off and pried Dad's lips apart . . . "Open your mouth and receive Jesus" to which he did, enough that I knew he had taken it in. We gave him water and he drank it promptly. His fever was still high and he was perspiring from time to time. He would kick off any blankets, and his lungs began to worry me. When he took a deep breath, I could hear rales and told Mom we needed to get him to the hospital, to which she agreed. She made a few phone calls and told other family members what the status was, then got her coat to leave.

Back to Mount Carmel. We followed the ambulance like bumper cars, close together so no one would get lost in the tangle of cars on the freeway.

My brothers Tom and Dave each drove their car and Mom rode with me. She was quiet and twisted her hankie in her hands.

"Mom, I think this will be the best for him. I am sure he is going into pneumonia . . . ." I began.

"Oh, I never thought we would be coming back here. I know they can help him more . . ." she trailed off and looked out the window.

". . . just so he doesn't suffer, Mom!"

Dad was admitted and we saw that he was comfortable before we left. The nurses and doctors hurried in and out of the room, listening to his lungs, etc.

I dropped Mom off, and then I went home to check on the children. John said he could take Monday off so I was relieved that I could spend more time with Mom, and Dad.

"Oh, yes, the Girl Scout Cookies, . . . ."

I gasped. I forgot all about them.

"Pat and Joe took them into their house and called the girls' parents to pick them up. All is OK".

Boy was I thankful, what wonderful neighbors and Annie, their daughter, is one of my Scouts.

Jim made it from Indianapolis, and Joe Robert was making arrangements to leave with his wife, Sara, and their children, Joseph, Julie, Thomas, and John, coming from Louisiana. Everyone else was close, and Sunday we took turns visiting with Mom and taking her to the cafeteria as she had not been eating well either. Dad was holding his own, no changes at all. Mom would not leave Dad that evening, so Dave, Jim, and I agreed to stay if she would go home and get some sleep.

"You will be better with a good night's sleep, and as long as we are here, we can call you if there is any change," I pled my case.

"OK, we will be back early tomorrow" Mom retorted.

A long night ensured as we turns sitting by my dad bedside and walking the halls. I found the chapel and cried my eyes out, glad to be alone for this flood of tears to finally burst forth. Just a little red light flickered in the chapel, eerily quiet.

Sure enough, mom and my sister Lois were back next morning. Jim drove and Dave and I returned to mom's home to sleep. The boys went downstairs to the spare beds there and I crawled into the hospital bed near the kitchen. I was almost asleep when the coo-coo clock began irritating clamor and I jumped up and stopped the hands, 7:00 before it could peep one more note!

Possibly around 10:30 Lois called us to come back to the hospital. I fixed a pot of coffee and the guys showered. Me, I could wait, I wanted to get there but was dependent on Jim to drive this morning.

Upon returning, nothing to my keen eye was different. Dad's output was lessening, his breathing was labored, and he didn't answer any of us when we talked to him.

John had summoned a good friend, a priest, to come see me at the hospital since John was busy taking care of the children. When Father Dan walked into the room, something came over me, which I could never explain to this day. We embraced and I asked Father Dan to pray with us that Dad would enter Heaven, this day.

"Why this day, Mary?" he asked.

"Today is the Feast of St. Joseph . . . his patron saint."

Father blessed Dad, and a calm came over me. I continued to pray, nothing more could be done. At about 6:45 I summoned everyone to Dad's bedside.

"What is it Mary?" Mom questioned me.

I explained that today was the Feast of St. Joseph and would be a Special Day in Heaven when Dad arrived.

We all gathered around and I began praying, I don't know what prayers I said, but we all encircled his bed as he took his last breath. "Thanks St. Joseph!"

At home we were sitting around with Father Dimond making arrangements for Dad's funeral Mass, when Mom looked up at the coo-coo clock and declared: "Look! The clock stopped at the same time Dad died!" Nothing more was said about that.

# Chapter 32

About this time, John's grandmother came to live with us. We gave her a bedroom and that had a sitting room (porch). We moved to the attic and I vividly recall that the first morning we woke up from sleeping in the attic we could both see our breath. Little nippy!

Grandmother was no problem for us. She had a phone in her room and was in communication with my mom and me from time to time. One time at dinner she seemed rather quiet so I asked her, "Grandmother, what is wrong, you are so quiet?"

She never complained. She told me she had a toothache, and believe it or not she had maybe eight teeth, so it was possible one had gone bad. No dentist would touch a 93 year old, so we ended up at Ohio State University Dental Emergency Clinic. I remember, a resident came to the door, looked around and centered his attention on Grandmother saying "1886?" No, it was not a mistake. We stood up and she had the tooth taken out with great delicate care.

John used to get Grandmother's coffee and toast in the morning and take it up to her. This way it was one less trip she had to make on the stairs. John was quite distressed as he would hear her praying "to die."

It was hard for to him to understand, but he continued to watch over her.

I found this poem and shared it with him.

### Life's Clock

The clock of life is wound but once,
And no man has the power
To tell just where the hands will stop
At late or early hour.

To lose one's wealth is sad indeed;
To lose one's health is more;
To lose one's soul is such a loss
That no man can restore.

The present only is our own,
Live, love, toil with a will—
Place no faith in "tomorrow"—for . . .
The clock may then be still.

\* \* \*

# Chapter 33

My children were in the first era of bussing. Cathy went to East High School and never missed a day in four years. John attended Immaculate Conception and when he was in the eight grade, a priest came to talk to them about becoming a priest, a missionary to be exact. He showed films and answered questions, passed out pamphlets and invited the boys to attend a week at their seminary high school in the summer. John was very excited about going, and of course we gave him permission.

    That week, John became more serious about wanting to attend the high school, PIME (Pontifical Institute for Missionaries). We were happy and I know in the back of my mind, I recalled the words of Mother Regina, "Some day you may have a child who will seek a religious vocation . . .". Her words would reverberate many times over in the next four years.

## "A Child's Night Prayer"

I say my prayers and hop into bed,
Straighten the pillow and smooth out the spread.

Someone is coming
You easily can see
To Dreamland we'll go
My Jesus and me.
Then mother Mary
With Jesus comes in,
We cover Him up
Right up to the chin,
And then we slip off
To the land of nod
Just wee little me
And the Son of God.

I found this prayer card in a book of John's and loved it very much. (Author Unknown)

Another favorite, "God is Good, All The Time" and you would repeat, "All The Time, God is Good"

John got excellent grades at PIME and lettered in basketball and soccer. He was far from a saint, however he was sought out for advice from his classmates.

One day, John and I decided to drive over to PIME (near Newark, Ohio, 25 miles east of Columbus) and donate a foosball table for the recreation area. When we got there, we knew something was afoot. When we finally asked where John was, the explanation, that he was put off the bus for acting up, did not set well with us. He was not the only one, but on this dark, rainy Saturday evening we were just concerned where he was and was he safe.

"He said if we didn't settle down he would stop the bus and we could get off . . . ." John said, once we found them, soaking wet, walking the berm of a two-lane road.

"No excuse! The four of you are Seniors and should have known better, and set an example for the others, and of course you know you have missed the evening meal," my husband chastised them.

"Yeah, we know!" John said. the other nodded in agreement.

"Want to go to McDonald's for a sandwich?" John asked and was met with cheers of joy, YEAH.

One day the rector, Father Dino, asked me, "Mrs. Dimond, do you know where John wants to do his missionary work later on?"

"No, he hasn't mentioned anything to us".

"He has shown an interest in Papua New Guinea, one of many missions we support".

I was stumped, ashen and completely speechless when I replied, "Oh, Father, he can't go there, I don't know where that is". He just chuckled and led me to a wall map and pointed out many of their mission lands.

John decided he wanted a more-rounded education, and I arranged a visit to Watterson High School for him. He loved it from the start, this being his Junior year. He got excellent grades at PIME (Seminary) and did very well at Watterson, where of course he "discovered girls" and began to date. Although he did not date Vickie in high school, she did graduate the same year and they later married.

# Chapter 34

I had taken a job to help pay bills and John's tuition, and although John wasn't for it, he finally came around and saw the benefits of my working. I was secretary to the president of a warehouse company but had nothing to do with the actually day to day business of the warehouse. When Tom, my boss, wasn't there, I found things to do to keep busy. One day I happened to answer the phone and the secretary of one of the largest distillers in Ohio asked me to ship out so much of their stock liquor.

I happened to have the most recent Accounts Receivable as I was organizing them and putting them in ledgers and labeling them with dates. I looked down at their particular account, and don't ask me why I asked it, but I remarked, "We need to get some money into this account before we could ship anything" and she cut me off, "What?" She put me on hold, and a minute later a very angry man was on the other end of that phone.

"What the hell are you talking about? Who are you? Where's Tommy?" he spoke fast and furiously.

"Tell him to call me ASAP," and he slammed the phone down.

Oh, God, I thought for a minute. No one calls Mr. Kaplin Tommy unless they really are friends. Oh boy, this is going to get me fired for sure. The minutes seemed endless until Tom walked in the door, greeting everyone and tossing his hat as if it were a basketball!

"2 points" he chimed, before turning to me, "what's up?"

"How well do you know Mr. Michelob?" (obviously not his real name).

He propped his feet up on his desk, leaned back and stretched, "Why, what's he want now?"

"He wants us to ship a large quantity of our stock and look here," as I opened the ledger on his desk. I only told his secretary that we would need to get some money before we ship . . . as you can see . . . ." I had to stop, practically stop breathing. He began looking at page after page. I was hoping that I had made a mistake and he would just call the man and assure him we would ship his merchandise. It was a very uneasy feeling.

"Get your calculator and add up his company's payments for the last six months." I wasn't sure I could concentrate enough to recognize them, let alone add them up. He was on the phone in a second assuring "Mr. Michelob" he was reviewing his account personally, and "after I fire my secretary, I'll get back with you".

I gulped hard. He turned the handset to the phone and winked at me, "Treat 'em with kindness."

"Are you really going to fire me?" Expecting some answer from him and not getting a reply, I continued adding the amounts.

"Mary, go get the bank deposit slips from Dale." Dale was the bookkeeper, and had been for a number of years. When I approached him for the slips he just began mumbling something about he had to put them in order first and he would get them together after he did something or other. I wasn't sure what it was but I could see he was visibly shaken.

"Dale, give them to me now. Mr. Kaplin wants them NOW." My job was probably up in the air at that moment. He opened a drawer and handed me deposit slips, in not such good order, but I hurried into Tom's office. We both began to run tabs on the deposit slips, and it wasn't too long when Tom said, "Mary, get Jack (he was the general manager) and bring Dale in here." He turned in his chair, put the calculator back in his drawer, and I left, still not knowing if I was wrong or not.

"Dale, Tom wants to see you . . . . NOW!" I raised my voice only to emphasize my nervousness and his lackadaisical attitude. He went directly then, and I followed him to my office. I shut the door and sat with my head in my hands mumbling a prayer. I don't know if I was praying not to get fired, or for Dale to forgive me for being nosy. Seconds passed.

"Mary, Tom wants you to take a statement," Jack hollered. I picked up my steno pad and pen and swiftly sat down in the room, not looking at anyone.

"Today is January, (something), and those in the room are, Jack G, general manager, my secretary, Mary, myself, president of Warehouse Services; and Dale H, bookkeeper. Now, Dale state your full name, and please repeat what you have previously admitted.

With pen poised to write, and only half hearing what I was about to hear . . .

"I, Dale H, admit to stealing . . . ."

"Stop" I said. Dale turned to look at me and Jack was shaking his head, but Tom looked at me with a sly look. "I guess you are learning something in that school after all. Dale, Mary is right, you have the right to have an attorney. Jack you will collect his keys and escort Dale off this property immediately."

With that I picked up my notebook and returned to my office, next door to Tom's. I noted he had shut his door, and I sat trembling and trying to pray. I was in shock. I couldn't believe what had just happened. I later learned this was "kiting," a form of a fake financial transaction: a negotiable bill, e.g. a check, that is fraudulently used to sustain credit or set up a bank account, by representing and using a fictitious name.

Moments later, Tom's wife stopped by. She noted his door was shut so she popped into my office, "Hey, who is in there with Tommy?" Immediately she saw that I had been crying. "Go on in, he's just having a private moment," I began.

"Poker party is more like it" she laughed. "Are you all right?" she asked. I nodded, she left and I heard her open Tom's door.

Later as I was leaving, he remarked "Now you have a new job . . . . the bookkeeper!" he grinned.

"Thanks a lot! . . . gotta go now, I have Criminal Justice to study tonight" and he waved goodbye as he answered his ever-ringing phone.

# Chapter 35

December, 1980 I had begun another possible career, a reserve policewoman for the City of Columbus. I attended the police classes two nights a week for 8 months, 6-10:00 PM. John didn't mind and he and Cathy spent quality time, and he helped her with her homework. I most always made dinner before I left for the academy.

Why would one want to be a police officer, and especially a female officer and not even get paid? Interestingly, Janet had left the convent several years after me and it was Janet who wanted to do this, but my husband wanted me to wait then until the children were older, so I waited. Janet was in the era of police women wearing skirts and carrying their gun in their purse!

Before you are sworn in there are many stringent steps, including a background investigation and a polygraph test. I didn't know what to expect but someone said the officer would leave the room, but really he was watching through a two-way mirror, so don't adjust your bra straps, etc. Also that the test could take as long as four hours, so "pee" before you go in there.

On July 11, 1979 was my appointment for the polygraph exam. The machine operator was an older man, a little "gruff," chewing on a stub of a cigar with a white shock of hair combed over an otherwise bald head. He put little "grippers" on my fingers and leads (long rubber tubes to measure respirations) around my chest.

"Feet flat on the floor. Do not interrupt me at any time, tell the truth at all times and answer "YES" or "NO," only! Got that?"

Away he bombarded me with questions.

"Have you ever stolen anything?"

"Yes" but would a candy bar count?

"Was it more than five dollars?" he asked

"No" a quick reply.

There were more questions regarding stealing, but it seemed pretty lame to even ask these questions.

The next battery of questions would refer to larceny and theft. He then turned in another direction.

"Have you ever taken money for a sex act?"

"NO!" I quickly answered and was blushing a cool pink.

"Have you ever performed a sex act for money?"

"NO" let's get on with this. I was beginning to feel like a criminal and yet I had nothing to do with this line of questioning.

"Have you ever had sex with an animal?" he nonchalantly asked.

I think I was beginning to unravel and wondered if he was making these up to purposely fail me.

"Absolutely NOT!" and he paused. Obviously those little needles were flying all over the graph paper he was watching.

"Have you ever used another name than that given on your application, except your maiden name?"

"Yes," I answered. Whew, at last we are on to some other type questions.

"Did you ever have checks or bank accounts in this name?"

"NO"

"Would anyone know you by this name?"

"Yes" I whispered.

"Does your husband know you used this name?"

Of course, and answered "Yes."

Things were just going nowhere, and all I could do was say Yes or No.

I thought he must have needed a potty break, I heard him shutting down his machine. He came around in front of me, put his two hands down on the desk, and stared me right in my eyes. I noted he was a little uneasy. I had a lump in my throat wondering what he was going to do next.

"What the hell was your name, Ms. Dimond?"

Without a mere hesitation, I blurted out, "Sister Mary Noel of the Holy Angels."

"Oh shit!" he declared and turned and went into an adjoining office. Well, I told the truth, what was his problem? I sat for a good 15 minutes before a Commander walked in and asked where the officer was who was performing the test.

"He left about 15 minutes ago, he went in that door . . ." I stammered. Was this part of the test? Was he watching me from a nearby window?

"I'll go see what's what" and he wandered out of the room. Moments later, he came in with a smirk on his face, began to unhook the wires from the machine.

"Is he all right?" I inquired.

"OH YES, he is back there holding his head, shaking it back and forth, mumbling,

"Oh my God" over and over, he laughed.

"Did I pass? Do I have to do this again?" but he interrupted, "No, I think you did better than him!"

In 1981 classes began at the police academy and you'd best never be late. The academy is run like a pseudo-military atmosphere. For instance, "Yes sir," "No sir," standing up when an instructor walked into the room, etc., (sort of like Catholic school). 344 hours of training were required for the Peace Officers Training Council's approval. We kept notebooks of our classes and they were graded. If something was missing, we had to make that class up. There were, I believe, six women in the class and a few guys who never served in the military so they knew as little as we did about these terms, like, dress right, dress left, ten hut, and about face, not to mention learning the ranking system of the officers, sergeants, lieutenants, captains, major, etc. We were taught when, where and how to salute, as protocol dictates. One of the first classes had just began when one of the females stood up, moved to the center aisle and preceded to leave the room.

"Excuse me, miss, have you been excused?" the officer at the podium bellowed out, not missing a beat of the class he was giving.

"I have to go to the little ladies' room" she replied.

"We don't have a little ladies' room" he retorted.

"Well, I have to pee" and she continued out the door.

Everything was geared toward men, policemen, but we were breaking into new territory and we were determined to be police officers no matter what our gender was. Another officer was putting on lipstick before the class began and as the sergeant turned at the podium to observe her, he said, "If you want to wear lipstick, then everyone will wear lipstick. Do you have enough to for all of us?"

She wiped her lips and blushing put her lipstick back in her pocket. We did not carry pocketbooks at all. Many of our classes were interesting, but some were just down right boring.

One day, a sergeant was going to teach us the proper way to respond to military formation. We all lined up, tallest in front, smallest in back, etc. He was giving us commands of "dress right" which meant stretch your right arm out to just barely touch the officer on your right, hence "dress right" and dress left was exactly as it was called. Parade rest was having your hands clasped behind your back, eyes front and feet apart. About face, meant a quick, spirited turn to face the front, or in some cases, face the back. "Ten hut" (never knew what or how that came about) meant ATTENTION. That we got! "At ease," was being in a relaxed mode but right foot firmly planted so you could quickly follow any other command that would follow. Being dismissed from rank would always follow "Attention", "troops dismissed."

The guys perhaps had been in the military so this was second nature to them, but the women, including me, had a hard time following these commands.

One day the sergeant became so frustrated with us all that he loudly proclaimed, "Take ten," and we did not know what that meant. We just stood and stared at him. He was seldom without his chaw of tobacco and a Coke can as his spittoon. He turned away, got rid of the chaw, and said even louder, "Take a break . . . take ten minutes . . . . get out of here . . . . move!" and we did . . . . quickly!

## LAW ENFORCEMENT CODE OF ETHICS

As a law enforcement officer, my fundamental duty is to serve mankind, to safeguard lives and property, to protect the innocent against deception, the weak against oppression or intimidation, and the peaceful against violence or disorder, and to respect the Constitutional right of all men to liberty, equality, and justice.

I will keep my private life unsullied as an example to all; maintain courageous calm in the face of danger, scorn, or ridicule; develop self-restraint and be constantly mindful of the welfare of others. Honest in thought and deed in both my personal and official life, I will be exemplary in obeying the laws of the land and the regulations of my department. Whatever I see or hear of a confidential nature or that is confided to me in my official capacity will be kept ever secret unless revelation is necessary in the performance of my duty.

I will never act officiously or permit personal feelings, prejudices, animosities or friendship to influence my decisions. With no compromise for crime and with relentless persecution of criminals, I will enforce the law courteously and appropriately without fear or favor, malice or ill will, never employing unnecessary force or violence and never accepting gratuities.

I recognize the badge of my office as a symbol of public trust to be held so long as I am true to the ethics of police service. I will constantly strive to achieve these objectives and ideals, dedicating myself before God to my chosen profession, law enforcement.

One of our classes was driving, and we went out in the parking lot and practiced stopping cars, searching cars, etc. It had been a beautiful warm day but it began to sprinkle and one officer (girl) proceeded to accelerate at the wrong time, skidding on the shiny black asphalt, right into a tree. She was going slow but the tires were bald and the car just slid. She wasn't hurt and of course "the ladies can't drive" reverberated through the academy.

Probably the least favorite of any officer who goes through the academy is the "gas house". 50 officers donned the face masks several times while the instructors made sure we had it right. 25 officers were led into a small garage-like structure and a foggy gas filled the room. You could hardly see a foot in front of you. We did good and walked back out. Next 25 went in, and we thought that was it. OH NO!

For the last part, we would enter the room again and when everyone was in . . . . take off the mask . . . and when given the signal, put it back on before we would be allowed to exit. Our eyes were burning, tears were rolling over our cheeks, our noses were, well no explanation needed. We made it in and back out intact. We just fell on the ground like wounded soldiers, tried to take deep breaths and finally took off our outer jackets which still had a faint smell of gas.

Firearms was a big part of our training and the guys looked forward to it. We learned to take apart the gun, clean it, and put it back together, and also how to use a shotgun. We practiced at the indoor range, outdoor range, and at a nearby quarry. We had set ways in which we would aim and fire, using right and left barricades, or lying on our stomach, all under the auspices of a sergeant.

The intense shooting took a toll on my right hand and I developed a cyst which became painful. I did have surgery to remove it and was back out on the range in no time. The sergeant had given me a little more time to qualify, but it came down to the last day I could even try.

"Dimond, let's go." he barked.

It was slightly raining and we headed out to the outdoor range. My hand was bandaged and I thought the padding would help me. This was my last chance as graduation day was approaching.

I began, at his command, "left barricade" and I aimed for the silhouetted target, emptied my weapon, pulled out a speed loader and refilled my 38 revolver as he loudly proclaimed, "right barricade."

Now really, there were just the two of us out there and he was inches behind me, leaning over my shoulder as I could smell his pungent chew.

Just as I got off the first two shots he put his hand on my shoulder, "STOP!"

"Now, what?" It was beginning to rain more and we both wore raincoats. He reached down and grabbed my right hand, "What the hell . . . . I thought it was healed?" He held my hand up with blood oozing through the gauze. I think I was near tears as he led me inside to his office. A nurse, he was NOT, but he unwrapped my hand, put something on it may have been just Vaseline, and rewrapped it in a very caring way. There was a soft side to this guy after all, but would he let me finish?

"Let's get it done," he motioned me to the door and back out in the rain. I almost forget to load my speed loaders, but he had to pack his jaw with tobacco, so I had an extra minute to get ready. As I said a quick "Hail Mary", took my stance and waited for the command to shoot . . . . the sun broke through and the rain stopped. He grinned at me and said, "How did you do that?" Without waiting for an answer, which I did not have, he ordered me to begin my last chance.

"Ready, prone position, 8 shots, center mass . . . ."

I dropped down in a muddy puddle and began pulling the trigger, . . . .

After what seemed an eternity, wet, cold, hand throbbing, (but not bleeding) I exhausted my ammo. He walked the length of the firing range and retrieved my target. I exhaled and followed the sergeant into the academy. He started circling the center mass and grading it with his black marker as I stood there dripping wet. I noticed how much gauze he had wrapped on my hand. It was a wonder I could even hold the gun.

"Good job, Dimond, you passed! Concentrate on squeezing the trigger . . . . slowly and you'll continue to do fine."

This was a big relief to me, probably the hardest thing in my career, so far!

One day we were told to stand in line and Officer Jack would be writing down how many belt keeps we wanted and measuring us for hats. Hmmm, belt keeps, I pondered. I asked the girl behind me, "How many belt things are you asking for?"

"Four," she said matter of factly.

I heard the guy in front of me ask for two, but I still wasn't sure what I even needed them for, so to be on the safe side, I asked for four.

Came the day that the belt keeps were passed out I finally understood why they were issued. A piece of leather, maybe six inches with snaps is put through your waist belt and then is also connected around your gun belt, thus keeping them together, securely. Of course I was glad I ordered four of them.

We had a schedule of what courses were held on which night. One evening we sat up straight with our book in front of us. Someone called, "Attention", and we rose, only to be told rather brusquely to "be seated". I nearly froze as I realized this class was on collection of evidence and polygraphs, understanding human behavior.

Our eyes met, only seconds after he began his repertoire; this was the officer that did my polygraph, but he wasn't chewing any chaw this time. He began to rattle off how important recruitment is in the police force and how women were making inroads in this field.

"Class, take ten, except" he then pointed to me, "I need to see you for a minute". Everyone filed out and gave me "funny" looks as he rifled through his papers.

"Mary Dimond, I recall," he began.

"Yes, sir."

"First I want to apologize for giving you such a hard time during your polygraph."

"Oh, I just thought it was a drill, to make me want to quit . . . ."

"I want to apologize for thinking the worst case scenario. I was definitely going in the wrong direction with you, and I have since changed my ways of interrogation. I now give people the benefit of the doubt and have become a little more charitable," he went on for another minute. He smiled and asked me to open the door so we could proceed with the class. Everyone was looking at me curiously, but silence in class took precedence.

Some of the courses we took were, The United States Constitution: Its provisions and Protections; Ethics, Courtesy and Discipline, Public Relations, Civil Rights Today; Laws of Arrest, Search and Evidence, Court Structure; Military Drill; Firearms Safety; Report Writing; learning the ten code and probably some I left out. The ten code is a numerical way officers respond to calls, 10-3 "Officer in Trouble" is most important and feared. It meant, either an officer was shot or was being overpowered and needed help, he was in immediate threat of death. All units (car and wagons) stopped what they were doing to respond to the 10-3.

We had spent 344 hours in class and now we prepared for graduation which took place August 4, 1981.

Everyone was excited to graduate and get on with the "police work" they had learned.

# Chapter 36

Wearing the uniform proudly and ready to patrol the streets of Columbus, one of my first assignments was with a freeway officer. Everyone knew him by "Rosie," but after 8 hours and putting over 400 miles on the odometer that one night, I called him "nuts". We traveled the freeway at break-neck speeds, lights and siren on which can really get the adrenaline pumping. He was everywhere, north, south, east, back north, far west, etc., and I was dizzy as a bat. He scribbled down things all the while he flashed his lights, ran the siren and most always was the first one at a scene, whether accident or just something in the freeway (junk). He was out of that cruiser in record-breaking time, mostly to see if an officer was all right.

I learned a lot that night; not to ride freeway if I had another choice.

I was still on "probation" so to speak; and working patrol with a male police officer. We were dispatched to the scene of an accident, and after checking to see that everyone was all right, my partner threw me a set of keys and said, "Get that car out of the intersection" pointing to a red automobile with damage to the rear end. Jumping at the chance to prove my worth, I got in the car, started the engine, discovered this was a standard transmission car. I did not know how to drive a standard car.

"Sir, I don't know how to drive a standard . . ." He was already busy with paperwork and getting the accident information from both parties involved.

"Just push the clutch in, shift and drive it . . . ." and he turned back to his clip board and was calling the license numbers in for validation.

I gave it another try and boy did that car "hop" another ten feet, out of the way of passing traffic. He never did say I did a good job; maybe he saw me, jumping it like a bunny.

Early in my career, there was a race in down-town Columbus, I mean "CAR" RACING. Buck Rinehart was Mayor at the time, and this was his baby. We were to patrol the areas which would pose potential risks to citizens (What about us?). The patrons would buy a wrist band that indicated where they were to watch the race. Red wrist bands allowed one to be in the pit zone; most were white for various stands or viewing sites.

As I was walking my "beat" I noticed a man with a young boy (perhaps his son) near the barricades. So I asked to see their wrist bands. The older gentleman wouldn't even look my way, the younger one tugged his dad's sleeve and said, "She wants to see our bands!"

"Please sir, if you do not have a red wrist band you will have to move." He did not show me his band, nor did he intend to move. Others around us began to notice. I radioed to the officer at the next post that I had a belligerent man, when the man turned and said, "Look I paid good money for this event and I will watch it wherever I want," and he turned to watch the warm up and I heard the roar of the engines. I could have shut the whole race down, but elected one more time to get him to move. At that time, we were issued a PR 24 which is a thick, black stick with a T-handle. I had never used it before but I felt it would be handy if the two of them ignored me much longer.

Dispatchers (radio) asked if I needed assistance since they had heard me talking to Officer Wells a minute before.

"Not at the moment. I do believe they are going to move," and I said it loud enough for them to hear. They walked away, shrugged their shoulders, and that was the last I saw of them.

A week later, Lieutenant Lewie of the academy called me due to a complaint they had gotten about me. I met him to go over the logistics of the complaint, and of course it was the man who had refused to move. He read me the letter and said he had had a meeting with the citizen. I assured him I did nothing wrong. I probably spent way to much time coaxing them to move on.

"Don't worry about this one; I had a meeting as I said with him. The very first thing he said to me was, "Women have no right to be cops!" and I politely ushered him out of my office. "You did right, but don't hesitate to call for help or even advice. That is what the sergeants are for, so use them."

Our son, John pinning on Dad's lieutenant badge

# Chapter 37

This may be a good time to review the "OFFICIAL TEN CODE—Columbus Division of Police (updated for this particular part, Feb, 2013.

| | |
|---|---|
| 10-3 | Officer in Trouble |
| 10-4 | Auto Accident |
| 10-4 A | Hit Skip |
| 10-5 | Auto Accident w/injury |
| 10-5A | Hit Skip w/injuries |
| 10-6 | Traffic Violator |
| 10-6 A | Auto Obstructing |
| 10-6 B | Auto Parking Violation |
| 10-7 | B&E / Burglary (Breaking and Entering) |
| 10-7 A | Building Open |
| 10-8 | B&E in progress |
| 10-8B | B&E in progress (vacant structure) |
| 10-8A | B&E Alarm |
| 10-9 | Bad Checks |
| 10-10 | Bomb Threat |
| 10-10A | Bomb Threat—Suspicious Package Found |

| | |
|---|---|
| 10-11 | Check for Stolen (usually car) |
| 10-12 | Check Registration (auto) |
| 10-13 | Check for Tickets (citizen previous tickets) |
| 10-14 | Cutting or Stabbing |
| 10-15 | Call Home (emergency call) |
| 10-16 | Disturbance |
| 10-16 A | Information/Assistance |
| 10-16B | Disturbance/Mental |
| 10-16C | Loud Noises |
| 10-16 F | Fireworks (complaint) |
| 10-17 | Domestic Violence |
| 10-17A | Domestic Dispute |
| 10-17B | Domestic Stand-by |
| 10-18 | DOA (dead on arrival) |
| 10-19 | Drunk |
| 10-20 | Drowning |
| 10-22 | Animal Complaint |
| 10-23 | Errand |
| 10-23A | Escort |
| 10-23 B | Lockout |
| 10-24 | Fire Squad |
| 10-24A | Infection/Contagious Disease |
| 10-25 | Fire |
| 10-25A | Trash Fire |
| 10-26 | Fight |
| 10-27 | Hospital/Assault Report |
| 10-27A | Telephone Harassment |
| 10-28 | Homicide |
| 10-29 | Juvenile |
| 10-30 | Larceny in Progress |
| 10-30A | Larceny Report |
| 10-30B | Shoplifter |
| 10-31 | Missing Person |

| | |
|---|---|
| 10-31A | Missing Person Returned |
| 10-32 | Message |
| 10-33 | Person with a Gun |
| 10-33A | Person with a Knife |
| 10-34 | Unknown Complaint |
| 10-34 A | Unknown Call/Panic Alarm |
| 10-34 B | 911 Hang UP Call |
| 10-34C | Check on Well Being |
| 10-35 | DUI (driving under the influence) (OVI current) Operating Vehicle impaired |
| 10-36 | Obstruction in the Street |
| 10-37 | Visitor/Official |
| 10-38 | Property Destruction in Progress |
| 10-38A | Property Destruction Report |
| 10-39 | Prowler |
| 10-40 | Recovered Property |
| 10-41 | Robbery just occurred |
| 10-41A | Old Robbery Report |
| 10-42 | Robbery in Progress |
| 10-42A | Robbery Alarm |
| 10-43 | Shooting |
| 10-43A | Shots Fired |
| 10-43B | Hunters |
| 10-44 | Sex Crime in Progress |
| 10-44 | Sex Crime Report |
| 10-44B | Indecent Exposure |
| 10-45 | Stolen Vehicle |
| 10-45A | Stolen Vehicle Recovered |
| 10-46 | Stranded |
| 10-47 | Suicide |
| 10-47 A | Suicide Attempt |
| 10-48 | Suspicious car |
| 10-48 A | Suspicious person |

| | |
|---|---|
| 10-48 B | Suspected Threat, Group Member or Activity |
| 10-49 | Vice Complaint |
| 10-49A | Narcotics Complaint |
| 10-50 | Wanted Person |
| 10-50A | Wanted Felon |
| 10-50B | Registered Felon |
| 10-51 | Wagon Run |
| 10-52 | Wrecker Run |
| 10-54 | Working Traffic |
| 10-55 | House Watch |
| 10-55 A | Park, Walk, Talk |
| 10-55B | Bail Bondsman |
| 10-56 | Request for Number (to complete report) |
| 10-57 | Request Assistance |
| 10-58 | Guard Duty (guarding prisoner in hospital) |
| 10-60 | Emergency Red Light/Siren |

These codes allow the officer to communicate with the dispatching officers, concisely, and eliminate a lot of "talk" on the radio. This is the radio code used on the police radio pertinent to Columbus; other departments, i.e. Highway Patrol, townships, bordering departments, Sherriff's Department may have other codes.

Also there are Clearance-Disposition Codes:

| | |
|---|---|
| Code 1 | Report and/or Citation |
| Code 2 | Party Advised or No Report Needed |
| Code 3 | Arrest Made |
| Code 4 | Non Arrest situation/Errand complete |
| | |
| Code 1 V | Report / Citation (video) |
| Code 2V | Party Advised / No Report needed |
| Code 3V | Arrest Made (video) |
| Code 4V | Non-Arrest Situation or Errand Completed |

The city is divided up into four zones, and each zone has various precincts. Each precinct has various numbers of cruisers depending on the number of residents, i.e., less in daylight hours and more in the evenings and weekends.

Follow me now: My partner and I were called to a 10-25, . . . 10-33 involved . . . . and 10-43. We were told to "60" it, per Lieutenant. We were buckled in and cautiously went through red light intersections. Our adrenaline was pumping and of all nights we had the shotgun (secured in the trunk of the car). The "60" was called off and Lieutenant made it a Code 3. When we got to the scene, Lieutenant gave us a quick rundown on what had happened. Someone had given him the gun that had been used in this crime, and Cheri and I proceeded to look for the spent shell casing. Finally he handed me the gun and five live bullets. Cheri told me to hold on to them. As we were dismissed from the scene, our next stop was the property room to turn the gun in. We took a deep breath and advised radio we were on a 10-23 (errand, if you are tired of looking it up). This was a 38 revolver I was holding. At the property room, I prepared to hand over the "goods" when the officer on the other side of the gated window, said, "What position were those bullets in the gun when it was given to you?"

A sinking feeling came over me.

"Here draw a diagram," handing me a pencil and pad of paper.

I looked at Cheri and together we opened the cylinder and began to "panic". We couldn't tell if the cylinder would turn clockwise or counter-clockwise. Luckily one of the firearms instructors I recognized came in the room and we quickly asked his advice. It didn't take more than a minute and we were able to hand in the gun, bullets and diagram to the property room officer. This shows the chain of command, that no one else had the gun but lieutenant and me (for when the time came to prove it in court).

I did work with another officer, Laura, who was an excellent role model and tough when necessary. We were dispatched to a fraternity house to take a report of some missing property.

We found the address and knocked on the door. A boy answered, took one look at us and remarked . . .

"I called for the police. Not women", he smirked.

Laura asked if he wanted to make a report or not, and he declined at that time.

Minutes later the sergeant called us and asked "Did you take a dispatch run to 44 East 14th Ave."

"We did. A boy that answered the door did not want to proceed with a report. So we left."

"Well, he is calling dispatch asking when a police officer was going to come make a report" and Laura interrupted. "Sir, we went there and he said he did not women officers, he wanted a police**man**."

Apparently the sergeant called him and told him he was out of line and he could go downtown tomorrow and file his report in person, since he was discourteous to his officers.

Another time I was assisting in a 10-26, and by the time we got there it was pretty much under control. We were told to "pat down" this 48-A. I was taking his wallet, some cards he had loose, and a wad of black "something" that looked like dog doo-doo, which I tossed on the dashboard. We made a quick report and itemized his belongings. We were on a run to the county with a man who possibly was 10-19, a 10-50, and possible 10-49. He almost went to sleep in the back seat. Cheri was driving, and I reached up on the dash and said to Cheri, "What do you suppose this is?"

She slowed down, turned the overhead light on and gasped "Where did that come from?" and I explained. I still didn't know what it was, but Cheri quietly said we would have to take it to the Property Room after we took the suspect to jail.

We woke our prisoner up and went into the sally port with him. For security purposed inside the jail, we locked up our weapons and deputies took our prisoner up to the desk for processing.

"Has he been patted down?" they asked us.

"Affirmative" Cheri responded.

They made him take off his shoes and as they pulled up his shirt to search his waistband, the deputy called out . . .

"Hell, this guy has bugs!"

We saw two of the bugs crawling their way up to his collar to hide in its folds. A deputy came out with a can of "disinfectant", and began spraying him down. Just then, Cheri gets the can and says, "Hell, we had him in the back seat of our cruiser" and out to the sally port she flew. She sprayed that back seat, probably using half the can then sprayed her feet and mine.

"Let's go, we can wash up at the sub", she said as the deputies threw us another can of "anti-bug" and laughed as we pulled out of the receiving bay.

"Cheri, what about this?" I said, holding the black "mystery item" up for her to see.

"Damn, we better get it to the property room" so we headed in that direction. The property room sergeant met us at the window, "What you girls got?" and we just smiled. We didn't know but we weren't going to tell him that.

"Here, I need an envelope to put it in," and laid it on the counter.

"Do you know what you have there?"

"Not exactly" and he said, "Smell it". Right, I was not about to touch it more than I needed to.

"Really, to prove what it is just smell it" he said.

Finally I picked it up, smelled it, and Cheri did too.

"Does it smell like grapes?" the sergeant said.

"By God it does, . . . . grapes, huh?" Cheri began.

"That is uncut heroin," and we just looked at each other.

"And to think I had it on the dash the whole time," I said as we filled out more paper work. A tag was put on it to "hold for narcotics," and the case number which was assigned. Someone along the way said this "black tar heroin" was worth over $5,000.

Well, we went back to the substation to again wash up and check our shoes, etc.

"Don't tell anyone about the 'visitors' we had, let's just keep mum on it."

Interesting note: the next shift officer put someone in the back seat the next day, and they almost slid across the seat and out the other door. Oops!

We were thinking of having our dinner, about 8:00 PM on a warm, summer night and just then radio summoned us.

"48, are you calling us?" (48 was our cruiser number)

I have a caller complaining of a strange smell

(there is no code for this complaint!) at 36 E Chittenden.

"Copy. OK, we will head that way." So dinner would wait. We were in the area where a lot of students lived, and as we approached the address we began to get a whiff of the complaint.

"Oh, God! I hope it's not a dead body" Cheri said, covering her nose with her handkerchief. As we walked up the steps we noted the window was not down and the screen was open a bit, allowing a very putrid smell to escape.

We went downstairs near the mailboxes and noted a number to call for any problems. As it happened, the man lived close by and said he would see us in a minute, which it was!

We all smelled this odor, and with his key he proceeded to open the door. Cheri pushed him aside, not that she was anxious to solve the mystery, but she was protecting him from any unwanted scene.

"Oh my God, look at this!" Cheri almost paled a color between Ivory and Snow!

There on the counter was a raw chicken as if someone was going to cut it up to cook. It had weird colors, and we would be permeated with this smell if we didn't get rid of it.

Cheri and I scooped it right onto a cookie sheet and into a garbage bag and headed outdoors to find a dumpster. The man located the girl who lived there; she had unexpectedly decided to go home for a visit. She had forgotten the chicken in her haste to leave. The man found some spray, but it did not even seem to put a dent in the smell. Last we saw, he was backing out of the door, still wildly spraying!

Another night we joined up with the narcotics unit. They had a house with suspected narcotics being sold so they asked us to back them up. I was familiar with the area, on a rather busy street, and we were going to surround the house.

"Dimond, Jennings, . . . . take the back" someone said in a hushed tone. Hands poised on our guns, ready to pounce on the first person we saw. The officer I was with, (not sure if it was Jennings, everyone is called by their last name), tossed his shotgun to me (lucky catch) and said "cover my ass," as he shinnied up the downspout to the porch roof. We waited and finally he came down saying, "They got them in the house".

I went in to see "the action" like you see on TV, and was immediately told,

"watch these kids!"

My heart went out to two small children seated on the couch. The parents were in the kitchen being questioned, patted down, and handcuffed.

I struck up a conversation with the children, noting there were no toys in sight, and little by little we began a dialog.

Sitting on the couch in front of us was a long coffee table with storage behind sliding doors. The little boy opened the door to get a small toy of some kind, when I spied scales. Funny place for scales, I thought.

"Sir, would you please ask the Sergeant in charge to come in here?"

"Yes, are these little tykes giving you some trouble?" He rubbed the little boy's head and winked at the little girl. Your Mommy and Daddy are fine, we will bring them in to see you in a few minutes . . . . now, Dimond, what did you want?"

"He took a little toy from the under the coffee table and I couldn't help but see a scale" He promptly turned the table around and began pulling out drug paranaphalia, baggies, and the scales, a rather large "bust".

The children were taken to Children's Services and my heart ached for them. They didn't even cry when their parents were escorted past them; perhaps they were too young to know what was happening.

I was riding with Cheri the night Officer Joe Rich was shot and killed. He had been on the freeway and picked up a citizen who would ultimately overpower him, get his gun, and shoot him. His cruiser that night did not have a "gate" (fence-like barrier between the front and back seat). We heard the transmission and then everything went dead. Cheri parked the car and tears rolled down her cheeks. She knew him far better than I, but nonetheless I had a lump in my throat.

All communication was silenced. An eerie pall fell over the whole city. Then, radio broadcast:

"Car 50, . . . Car 50 can you respond? Silence. We could hardly breathe. Then: "Car 50—out of service, Officer Rich has gone to Heaven" . . . . sirens wailed! It was a somber evening as we gathered at the sub station for the details.

There is nothing more touching or heart wrenching that laying an officer to rest. Badges are covered with a black stripe of tape, flags are at half staff. Officer Rich's service was held at a church where we officers stood on the front lawn in our best uniform (subject to inspection). The services were broadcast to us outside and the cortege of cars to the cemetery was endless. The honor guard stood at attention, the helicopters buzzed above us, a riderless horse with boots turned backwards in the stirrups, all played out in this theater of events to say farewell to a well-liked officer, husband and father. A 21 gun salute jolted us back to realization of this tragic event.

One girl and a situation I can never forget was an eye opening experience for me. We were patrolling the area around OSU campus and it was a relatively quiet night. We were thinking of getting something to eat, but about that time dispatch called us on a 10-44A (which is a report of a sex crime). We went to the address given and it seemed forever before a young college girl answered the door. She returned to her "nesting" area and covered up with a blanket. My partner, Cheri began to ask questions and the girl wouldn't even look at her.

"Have you been raped?" she quizzed her.

"I don't know . . ." and began sobbing in a tissue.'

"Either you have or haven't . . . you're old enough to know." My partner became exasperated. She went to get something from the cruiser and I sat down on the couch, pushing some laundry aside, and began to talk to this young girl.

"Honey, we are here to help you. Do you need to go to the hospital?"

"No," she replied.

"Are you hurt? Did someone hurt you?" I plied.

Before Cheri came back in the girl said, "the guy downstairs followed me up here when I came from the Laundromat" she was still whimpering.

"Did he hurt you?" I again asked.

The girl wiped her eyes, blew her nose and clutched her cell phone, and after what seemed like a long time before she answered, "Yes.

"I think you are hurting" I told her. "Please, we are going to have to go, so if you want us to help you, please tell us the truth."

"Well, he was pulling at my clothes and said things I don't want to repeat, but he had every intention to rape me . . . I told him I had VD, thinking that would keep him away from me, but he . . . ." again sobs and blowing her nose.

"It's OK, we have heard it all. We only want to do what is right by you," Cheri softened.

"Well, we had pizza last night and my boyfriend left early this morning and I didn't clean up . . . the boxes, the beer bottles and the . . . . Tabasco sauce were strewn about" she sobbed. He picked up the bottle and tried to shove it . . . ." uncontrolled sobs and hysteria.

"OK, you need to go to the hospital. We need to arrest this man, and pursue charges of Sexual Imposition/Sexual Battery. If we bring him up here, will you identify him?"

"I'm calling a friend first. She can take me to the hospital . . . . ok, I will show you where he lives," and proceeded down the metal staircase. The victim stayed off to the side with me while Cheri questioned the young man. I signaled Cheri that we had a positive ID on him. She then put him in handcuffs and into the backseat of our cruiser.

These are the heinous crimes, the scum that roam the earth that officers try to be delicate about, yet they fire up our innermost feelings of hate and loathsomeness for these perpetrators.

John joined the department in 1985, right after he had to have his gall bladder out. He was President of his class and enjoyed working the same shift as me. Reserve officers work with a regular officer, and have all the rights and responsibilities, must uphold the law and be professional at all times. There are a few times that Reserves work together, i.e. Halloween Patrol, etc.

One time, John and I were working together and he was driving the cruiser. It was a dark, rainy night and we were getting ready to mark off (quit) for the night. Heading west on the freeway we unexpectedly ran over something. We looked at each other, what was that? No, it was not a pot hole, this "something" tipped the cruiser precariously, so John decided to pull off the freeway, backup, and see if we could find out what it was. Another car stopped after us and said he thought he ran over someone. My stomach was queasy as we walked back to identify what we ran over. Cars were slowing down, and John asked the man to return to his car for safety reasons. As we approached the area, we noted a large roll of carpet. It took all our might to get that carpet off the freeway that night. Thank God it wasn't what we thought it might be, (a body).

As you can see by now, not all police work is guns and fights. Recently at Cheri's retirement dinner we fondly recall this incident:

One evening we both arrived at the precinct (#4) and Sergeant Johnson was in his office and we spoke to him.

"Where might the girls be having dinner this evening?" he remarked.

Cheri and I both looked at each other and shrugged our shoulders.

"The chicken place will close at midnight. Does that sound good?"

"Of course," we both replied.

He wanted us to pick up something for him there too, so he gave us his order and paid for all of it, and we left to go get it. We returned shortly with three bags of chicken, cole slaw, mashed potatoes, corn, the whole bit. Officer Mike saw us coming in with the food and asked, "Hey, chicken! Was that free?"

"Yep" and we turned to the kitchen area and set it on the counter.

"Really, free?" he just looked at the food and said to me, "Did you pay for that?" and I quickly said "No".

He was out the door in minutes and Sgt. Johnson was into the bags in no time. Cheri picked up her mail and we retrieved the shotgun, so we were about to leave the sub station, when we heard the awfully loud footsteps of none other than Mike. He was grumbling and had two bags obviously full of chicken.

"Hey, you said it was free and I got all this stuff and I didn't have enough money . . . ."

"Mine was free, wasn't yours Mary?" and we passed him, getting outside and in the cruiser (fast). We heard later that Sgt. Johnson "loaned" him the money so he could go back and pay for his dinner.

Another time we were answering a call and the fire department had gotten there before us. I believe it was a garage fire and the alley was rather narrow. Cheri decided to drive over the firemen's hoses in the alley rather than back up the whole block and go around. As we "humped" over the hoses there was an obvious lull in the water pressure, twice (front tires and rear tires). We both got out and went to speak to the resident and get a report. When we came back Cheri and I opened our doors almost simultaneously and both exploded with expletives! Our famous firefighters had filled the wheel wells of our cruiser with water! It was no small task scooping the water out with coffee cups, and all while the culprits looked on. "Don't mess with us . . . never ever run over our hoses!" they called as they drove away.

Speaking of alleys . . . Cheri and I were dispatched to a possible 10-16, 10-34 and 10-39 in an alley. (That is, disturbance, complaint unknown and possible prowler). Most of the cars were tied up on our precinct, and it was 2:00 in the morning. We proceeded to the location but there are no numbers in the back of these homes so we asked the radio dispatcher to have the homeowner (complainant) to turn on her back porch light. Sure enough, we were very close and cautiously got out of the cruiser, guns drawn. Cheri decided to take the rear, (figuring that if there was someone in there, they would most likely take the back way out). As we got close, we could hear "sounds" and metal. Again, Cheri asked radio to ask the homeowner if there was a car in the garage, and "negative" promptly came back. Not wanting to waste any more time, she told me to kick in the door and be ready to face "what ever," and I did . . . . the biggest opossum I had ever seen eating out of a metal garbage can that was tipped-over.

# Chapter 38

Juggling my job, being a police officer part time, handing the duties of running a house, and caring for two teenagers was quite a handful at times.

One time, John and I were in bed on the third floor and we were awakened by footsteps coming up the stairs. I don't know who spoke first, but John asked, "Dad, do you have any condoms?" . . . . that pause was unbearable.

"No, John, and we need to talk about this" my husband said.

"Oh, they are not for me, but for Sam." his high school friend.

I had also been involved in a disturbance call, teenagers drinking, loud music, etc. When we entered the open door, my partner, Officer Erickson yelled, "Down on the floor, back up to the wall . . . don't talk, turn that music off, provide proof of age, and if you are holding a beer bottle, glass, whatever, set it down next to you".

We were clearly outnumbered but they obeyed very well. As I began looking at I.D.'s and making a list, I asked, "where do you go to school?" With some careful thought and consideration I learned that some of them were classmates of John's. Good Catholic boys and girls who were caught up in this vice of drinking, and many were hesitant to call their parents.

"Would you like me to call your principal, Mr. Durant? I'm sure he would be glad to give you a ride home!"

The looks on their faces said it all. They became ashen and relaxed as if they were giving up.

I was given permission by Erickson to start sorting through the "suspects," and if no alcohol was present to let them go, finding out and writing down how they were getting home, who was driving, etc.

As they were being dismissed one by one, a boy asked me, "Are you John Dimond's mother?"

I had never been speechless! I quietly leaned over and whispered, "Yes, and there will be no retaliation. Why don't you just sit here for a few minutes and think about it?" as I ushered him to a corner where I could watch him wiggle and squirm.

My husband, John began the academy on March 11, 1985 which actually was his birthday. I had to drive him to classes since he was prohibited from driving due to his recent gallbladder surgery. He went four nights a week, accumulating 344 hours of training to satisfy the City and State requirements.

His classes were pretty much the same as mine but he was used to the military regime, having been in the Navy (or did I mention that?) John was elected President of his class. He enjoyed, and still enjoys, the firearms part. I was always interested in what class he was having and topics that they covered. To this day, he is very organized and keeps his code books up to date, attends monthly meetings, etc.

I remember being in a ladies restroom one time and obviously not alone. A mother had brought her daughter into the stall with her and for some unknown reason she looked under the partition to where I was.

"Honey, don't do that, that is not nice . . ."

"But Mommy, those are men's shoes . . . and I quickly piped up with, "I'm a policewoman and have to wear these funny shoes!" End of story.

# Chapter 39

About this time, we received a call from the President of the Bank in Indiana where Grandmother's sister lived. Etta was a bit younger and had a nice comfortable home and lived on a pension. The man asked us, if we could come see to Mrs. Smith's affairs. He was not permitted to give any details. I called Aunt Curly, (what she was always called), and she answered the phone. "We were planning to bring Grandmother over for a visit tomorrow (Sunday) if you would like company," I said.

"Oh, I'll fix a pork roast and would love to see all of you", so our plans were finalized. My mother watched our two children and we left early Sunday with Grandmother in tow.

When we approached the house, it was dark! The door was locked and no sign of anyone. I went next door to see if they had seen Aunt Curly recently, since I had just talked to her.

"Oh, thank God, you are here to help that poor lady. She is surely in a heap of trouble . . . .".

She invited us in and offered us drinks., and began a woeful tale of how Aunt Curly had a young man do some work on her roof and he continued to come around. She would buy him beer and they would go away at times. "She bought him a car . . . see here I have the papers . . ." this kind lady could hardly tell us fast enough.

"Let's call the police" I exclaimed.

They arrived shortly and we explained that I talked to her yesterday, had come from Columbus, and brought her sister pointing to Grandmother on the couch.

"Well, Mr. Dimond, let's go see if we can get in the house" . . . .

"Here I have a key, had it for years; I sure hope it still fits."

I was miffed! I'm the policewoman here and have as much right to inspect the house also . . . but I waited for them to call me.

There was hardly any furniture, kitchen appliances, or plates and silverware. There were two bottles of beer in the refrigerator, and a stick of butter. Now I was beginning to see the picture.

"Come, look at this . . ." the officer called to us.

In the bathroom, on the floor were drops of blood and what appeared to be a lens perhaps from her glasses.

The officer picked it up and put it in an envelope, and we told him that the neighbor had some papers for an automobile that Aunt Curly bought the young man so we went back over there to investigate more thoroughly.

The neighbor had been keeping mail since she knew Aunt Curly was 'drunk' most of the time, and she did not want this young man to have access to any of her things. The officer looked through the papers and announced, "I'll run this tag and see who it comes back to" he began. "Dispatch, I need the validation of license such and such . . . . ok, thanks". Within minutes he knew the individual and had an address for him. We waited there for further word.

"OH MY GOD!" I gasped as I saw Aunt Curly being hoisted up beneath her arms, trying to walk, hair straight up, and she was trying to kiss one of the officers! They brought her in and Grandmother was so distraught at seeing her this way.

"What now?" John said.

"Let's take her to the hospital and get her checked out, OK Aunt Curly?" I said. She was intoxicated and her breath revealed she had imbibed quite recently. Unfortunately, the hospital would not keep her just because she was intoxicated, unless I sat with her. We had an appointment the next day at the bank, and would pay the police a visit and let them know what plans we had made for Aunt Curly.

The neighbors invited us to stay there but John and grandmother got a room at a nearby hotel. There was no way we could have stayed at Aunt Curly's; was in shambles.

I spent the night in Aunt Curly's room at the hospital, but I did not sit. She wanted to "go somewhere", get a beer, find her man", and so it went, 2-3-4-6AM, and finally she closed her eyes and slept peacefully.

John came early and Grandmother stayed with the neighbor lady while we went to the bank.

"Thank you for coming, Mr. and Mrs. Dimond; I appreciate your help.

"Aunt Curly has always been independent and we know nothing about her finances" we began.

"OK, she comes in here and requests $500 to $5000 at a time, I should say demands loudly, and her gentleman friend is always with her. She most often is intoxicated, and we are just concerned that the guy is taking advantage of her".

"Well, she is in the hospital under protective custody so 'he' can't see her, and we are going to the police department next to apprise them of the situation".

"Good, shall we put a hold on her accounts?" and we agreed. He also advised us that **if she would** agree to it, they could put her into a trust where the bank would disburse her funds in a lawful manner, and perhaps get her into a nursing home.

"That would be great" we agreed. We didn't know if she had a will, what her finances were or anything, but he agreed to go with us to the hospital and get her to sign the papers. We went that afternoon and met with a social worker and explained what we were going to do. She agreed to witness the transaction, and said we should talk to the doctor before we left.

It was an "Act of God" that she signed the papers, as she recognized the 'bank man,' as she called him. She needed medical care, so we would leave her there until the trust officer was appointed and took over. As it turned out she had breast cancer and had to have surgery before she was moved to a very nice nursing home.

We visited several times after that although she did not know us. One time, we went into the room and she was somewhat startled when we called her "Aunt Curly" (seemed to jolt her memory). John pointed to a picture on the nightstand, "Who is that?"

I did not recognize the picture, so when one of the nurses came in we asked if she knew who that was, pointing to the picture.

"Oh, just to make it seem homey we put pictures in each room, probably from someone who has passed away", and that was 'homey' I thought!

Aunt Curly was born Etta Jane Billger, September 26, 1893, seven years after Grandmother.

Unfortunately, this "*homey*" nursing center *lost our names* and we were not notified of her passing.

# Chapter 40

John graduated from the Academy in July, 1985, and we began working 4 precinct together, but in separate cruisers usually with different partners each night. One particular day, a Saturday, Charlene and I were dispatched to a location where a car was blocking an alley. The residents were complaining because the trash collectors couldn't get down the alley. First, we ran the plates (called dispatch to run the tags and see who owns the car), which were not registered to this make of car. No one came out to claim ownership, so Charlene wrote out the ticket and I put in under the windshield wiper. She then called for a wrecker, planning to have it towed it to the police impound lot.

As soon as the wrecker arrived, a man came out of a nearby apartment, obviously he just woke up.

"Leave my f . . . ing car alone, get away and take that ticket with you!" he began a tirade of complaints with every swear word he knew. Charlene called our sergeant and apprised him of the situation. Within minutes, he showed up.

We offered to push the car out of the way, but he could not show us ownership and became hostile. He took a swing at the sergeant, and as they say, "all hell broke loose". Sergeant immediately put out a 10-3 (officer in trouble), and John and Hal, his partner that day, were at the substation having lunch when this dispatch went out.

"Hey, we better get down there and see what is going on? Is Mary working with Charlene? I know they took the initial call." and they grabbed their hats and headed to the scene.

"Not very often does a sergeant put out a 10-3" Hal said, especially on a Saturday at noon.

Within minutes, a scrappy 'kid' with a ball cap and dirty sweats, pushed me aside and jumped on the perp and brought him down. Sergeant called this "kid" by name and I found out he was a member of the SWAT team (Special Weapons and Tactics).

A lady came out of the apartment, yelling "Leave him alone. I'll help you Charles."

"Please lady, get back or you will get hurt," as I was picking up our walkies, hats and Char's watch which had taken a beating and landed on the ground beneath our feet.

She kept approaching the scene and the next thing I knew she swung and hit me in the face, breaking my glasses. No more *nice* policewoman, I grabbed her with my fingernails by the throat and had her on her tiptoes. More SWAT officers had arrived and had the man in the back of a cruiser. One of them came over to us.

"Hey Dimond, what's up?"

"She swung and hit me, broke my glasses and . . ."

With that he took her into custody, charged her with Assault on a Police Officer, and put her in another cruiser.

Lieutenant came over and insisted I go and get my eyes washed out while they cleaned up the paper work and the scene, towing the car, etc.

John came over finally to see if I was all right and after assuring him I was fine, Charlene and I left to wash my eye and get lunch, in that order. The woman ended up having to pay for my eyeglasses, and I had a black eye to explain for a week or more.

# Chapter 41

Sometimes we rode night shift 10-6 AM. John rode with Joel and I rode with Charlene or Cheri. We always had to catch up with each other as we settled into the shift, chatting and laughing, but always with an ear on the radio.

"Cars on 4 precinct, be alert for a tall, white male, wearing a red OSU jersey, grey sweatpants, and a black hat (everyone in this area could match this description). He just threw a brick through a window at 1976 North High Street." Since we were in the area, we continued southbound on High Street.

"Cheri that's him!" I clamored as I began to get out of the seat belt.

Cheri called in our L (location) and that we had a possible suspect.

"Don't slam the door when you get out, I'm going to get as close as I can . . ." Cheri remarked.

With that, we were out of the cruiser and approached the guy who apparently had been running quite awhile.

"You're under arrest," Cherie advised this man, and we began to get his arms behind him. We had one handcuff on him, and went to the ground wrestling to get the other hand cuffed.

I looked up to see about ten of his friends running towards us, yelling, "get off our friend, he didn't do anything."

With that, my worse fears rose to make me really angry. "Get the F . . . out of here all of you or you all will go to jail!" I blasted my words like venom from a snake. Cheri was fumbling with the handcuffs. I thought we would lose him, but the guys, (his rugby team friends) all stopped and watched us continue to wrestle with their buddy.

After we had him in the back seat, I looked at Sherrie and asked, "What were you thinking? We almost lost him . . . ."

She was almost giggling, but I did not see the humor in this situation.

"Uh hum, I heard somewhere that you used to be a nun, is that correct?"

And I answered affirmative.

"Well, I've never heard you say shit, and you come out with the F word!!!" We both laughed and transported our "jail bird" downtown to the slammer.

# Chapter 42

Police duty can be mundane one minute and exciting the next, all in a shift. Usually when John and I would get off duty at 6 in the morning we would have breakfast at an all-night diner. One morning, I was waiting on him; ten minutes passed and I asked the sergeant if he knew where they were or had they been dispatched late?

He shrugged his shoulders and picked up his walkie to call them, which I could do except this was not appropriate transmission for the walkie. Other officers were coming in to begin their shift. Just then, John and his partner walked in.

I was about to ask him where he had been so long, when I noticed powdered sugar all over the front of his uniform pants. Without thinking, I began to brush the powder off, and within seconds other officers were lining up to get "dusted off." I turned every shade of red there is and left in a hurry.

One time we went to the diner after 7:00 A.M., and of course it was open so we went in, poured our coffee, picked up a paper, and began to read it. We were getting refills, and I asked John to check and see where the waiter/owner was and laughed, "should I begin to fix our eggs?"

"I woke him up!" John said when he returned. He was so embarrassed as he took our orders and said, "Thanks for keeping an eye on things for me." We laughed and he wouldn't even accept a tip that morning.

I want to share the Mission Statement of the Columbus Ohio Division of Police:

*We the men and women of the Columbus Division of Police are dedicated to improving the quality of life in our City by enhancing public safety through cooperative interaction with our community and with other public and private agencies.*

*We are committed to reducing fear by maintaining order and peace.*

*We are responsible for protecting life and property, enforcing laws and taking all appropriate measures to combat crime.*

*We are organized, staffed, and trained to maximize effective and efficient public service and to maintain a positive work environment.*

*We work to fulfill the mission of the Columbus Division of Police in a manner that inspires the public's trust and confidence and protects the Constitutional rights of each citizen.*

\* \* \*

# Chapter 43

One day, my mother called me at work and said Grandmother had fallen. I raced home to find her still in bed and in pain. I called a squad and at the emergency room we found out she had cracked her pelvis. From then on she had to be in a nursing home, one that was close to where I worked. She got terrific care and enjoyed the activities once her pelvis began to knit and heal. I saw her every night on my way home and the family would see her on weekends. Truthfully, she was not happy but at her age 98 it was best for her.

One night, several years later, on the way home from work, I stopped to see her and pick up her laundry, which I did weekly. Her food was sitting in front of her but the nurse said she was too tired to eat, so I quietly left.

At home, I would start the washing machine and add detergent and a whole lot of bleach before throwing in her clothes. This night I was horrified to see a lot of blood on her clothes . . . what is this? I called the nursing home and talked to the head nurse, "What is this blood on her clothes?" I asked.

"Well, you know she has hemorrhoids . . ."

I cut her off, "this is more than that . . . please have her transported to the emergency room. Grant Hospital is fine, and I will be there."

John finished fixing dinner and helped the children with their homework, and I went to Grant Hospital. They had already assessed her and she was lying on the cart but she knew me.

"We think she has some abdominal bleeding and we would like permission to operate . . ."

"What?" I couldn't believe what I was hearing. "No, I would not put anyone through an operation at 98 years old, positively not . . . . where is the doctor?"

"Well we were thinking of putting in a shunt so we can medicate her." I wasn't even listening at this point but they assured me this was the way to go.

I stood near her bed but she seemed to be going downhill fast. I found a stepstool to get closer to her so I could hear if she spoke, and hovered nearby.

"Grandmother, do you want to go to Heaven?"

Nothing.

"Grandmother, do you want to see Catherine? You know she is in Heaven."

With that a smile came over her face and possibly a nod. A nurse came in and checked her vitals and a priest appeared next. She was gone, that quick. As the priest prayed, I stood stoic, not quite sure why I had not called John; after all, this was his grandmother.

She had a beautiful service at which Father Dimond presided. No tears were shed, as she had led a long, long life. One time our son John had figured out how many presidents she had lived through, from 1886 to 1984; 19 in all!

# Chapter 44

Cathy (Catherine Marie Dimond), our daughter was married on July 1, 1989, to Douglas Dillon, her high school sweetheart. They moved to California since Doug was serving in the Navy aboard the USS Independence.

One day we got a call that Cathy was pregnant with twins. How excited we all were! She would be coming home, as Doug would be shipped out for the Desert Storm War which was about to take place.

By this time the twins were six weeks old and we were excited about being grandparents for the first time! We had been to the academy to qualify in firearms (required four times a year). Before going to meet Cathy at the airport, and in a hurry to get there, I forgot I had six bullets in my pants pocket.

Going through the metal detectors at the airport, of course I sounded the alarm. I nearly died when I reached in my pocket and realized my 'crime' of error. John was beside me and we tried to explain where we had just come from and that we had locked our weapons in our car trunk. He sighed, "Prove you are police officers?" and we were able to produce our I.D.'s and he allowed us to go through. He followed me to a locker where I put the bullets for the time being.

Cathy was last off the airplane accompanied by three stewardesses who helped with the babies, car seats, diaper bags, etc. They were so precious, and we just marveled at God's handiwork. They were indeed identical and the picture of health.

Cathy and the twins moved in with us. I had spent months getting the nursery ready for them. Two beds, diaper changing table, dressers, swings, extra carriers, etc; we had it all!

Our first grandson, Jeff, was born on May 12, 1992, and Doug was out of the service by now.

About this time John, our son, joined the Marines. He loved the Marines and especially ordnance (rifle range) where he took top honors in his platoon, scoring 234 for High Shooter. He received the *Leatherneck Magazine* for rifle marksmanship proficiency. He was stationed in Okinawa. From his graduation program, I noted: "*Among all the honors, among all the postings, promotion, medals, that have been awarded me, the one in which I take most pride is to able to say,—*
*I AM A MARINE.*"

General John A. Lejeune, USMC 13th Commandant. I believe this is who the camp was named after at Parris Island, So. Carolina.

John married Vickie Petrelli, who had also gone to Watterson, on May 16, 1992. After they married, John was stationed at Twenty Nine Palms, California where they lived when their first baby, John Joseph III, (Jay, we called him) was born. Since John married a girl with a very Italian name he wanted to know more about his heritage, namely his father's. My husband John had always been told he was adopted as was his sister, Janet.

John and Janet's father became ill and had surgery at Ohio State University for esophageal cancer. He had smoked a great deal of his lifetime, so it was no surprise that he was afflicted with this horrible cancer.

Towards the end of his days on earth, he was moved to a nursing home in New Lexington, Ohio, where he had spent the first 20 some years of his life.

It was obvious to Janet and me that he was nearing death, so together our Catholic nursing took over. We changed his bed, rolling him from side to side, bathed him and put fresh clothes on him. This man was a pillar of strength and always cared about you and your children, and never complained of his condition. He was a tremendous father-in-law; we loved him dearly. He died that night after we had left, May 9, 1993. Of course Father Dimond said the Mass and presided at the burial which was in the family plot in New Lexington.

# Chapter 45

In October, 1994, John moved his family back to Ohio, and still wanted to know about his roots. To begin the search, John Sr., had to request a copy of his birth certificate, which we obtained, showing the correct spelling of his biological mother's name. We went to the Ohio Historical Society where we searched the name and found several in the Columbus area.

We sat in our kitchen, just hoping this search would pay off. I began calling people with the same name, and I said I was doing a genealogy study on the Miceli name. This woman was very helpful and said her dad was Tony Miceli, one of 11 children. They lived on 14th Avenue, which was the address on the birth certificate, so we felt certain we were on the right track. She went through the names of the family and told us if they were living, if so, in good health, etc. We went through eight names before she said "Then there is Annie." HOT DOG!!

Although she was in Mount Carmel Hospital due to the fact she had diabetes and was having dialysis, I called the hospital and was connected to her room.

"Mrs. Morris" (she had married Leon Morris, when she got word that the baby's father, Tony was lost at sea).

"Yes," she sounded sleepy.

"Would you want to know something that took place in your life in 1944?" I could hardly speak. We waited.

"No" she said. We were crushed. I said goodbye and hung up. What a bummer! We had tried so long, and now we were stopped in our tracks.

It was quiet the rest of the weekend.

Little did we know, after John's evening class at college, he went over to Mount Carmel and spoke to the nurse on the dialysis floor.

"She is my grandmother, we want an opportunity to get to know her . . . would it be all right if I talk with her?" Apparently yesterday she had had a bad day and was confused and probably did not know what we wanted, the nurse told John.

He went in and pulled up a chair and began to talk generally with her. He could dish it out . . . he was good at that. After an hour or so, she asked him,

"What do you do here at the hospital?"

John took a deep breath, pulled the chair closer to her bedside.

"I'm your grandson!"

Another hour of questions and answers ensued, and John could hardly get away to get home and tell us she wanted to meet "all of us."

It was a most endearing meeting. She was glad that John had been raised Catholic and attended Catholic schools. She, of course, married Leon and they never had any children, but she loved her many nieces and nephews. She lived in Grandview, which was just blocks away from where John worked at Abex for 27 years.

We went to the hospital after visiting hours. Since no one in her family knew of his birth, one can only imagine the smile on her face when John approached her, giving her a hug.

We began to meet the family, and as Annie's condition deteriorated, we were there beside her bed. She smiled so widely when she saw John in his police uniform. He had worked an event at the airport and they called the police department to get him there. "His mother is dying."

I heard her trying to say something and no one could understand what she wanted. I got near to her and was able to interpret what she wanted.

"Sister Marie, Father Smith" was barely audible. Interestingly we knew these two people, a nun and a priest, who had been assigned to our parish after they worked at St. Christopher's, which was Annie's parish. They all played cards together and she wanted them there. She felt it was time.

They arrived and did a double take when they saw us. What's the connection? I don't think she ever told them about her baby in 1944, and how awful it must have been to give this baby boy up for adoption.

We all joined Father as he said some prayers. Her rosary was constantly in her fingers and no doubt, a prayer on her lips. I approached to say, "good night," and I could sense she was hurting.

"Annie, do you want to go to Heaven? It's OK, let go, be at peace, . . . . the angels will meet you at Heaven's door" and I felt so good when she responded with a smile.

Annie went to Heaven an hour after we left.

This is a very sad time, but children always put a smile on our faces at times like this. We had taken the twins to the funeral home for viewing as they all wanted to get to know our family. It was very crowded, and John was busy meeting his aunts and uncles he had never known.

I decided to let the twins see her up close since there was a lull in the line that had snaked through the room all night long. We went up and I knelt on the predieu while they stood on it to get a closer look. They were just two, but very smart. The casket was surrounded with beautiful flowers. She wore a beautiful blue gown and of course her rosary was wound around her fingers. Her hair was coiffed and every hair in place, stunning silver.

"Do you know who this is?" I quietly asked them. They both shook their heads.

"Who is this?" trying to coax an answer of great grandmother from them.

They looked at each other, and one of them stated: "Snow White." I laughed quietly as we went back to our seats. How precious, how innocent!

# Chapter 46

My nephew, Kevin Myers, joined the police department at this time and has enjoyed a multi-career including patrol, crime scene investigation, and marine patrol, to name a few. I recall how ornery he was as a little boy, and couldn't fathom the idea of him, a cop!

John and Vickie had another child, a girl, Marissa. Our family had grown when Cathy announced they were expecting, again. This would be Patrick Douglas, a blonde haired cutie.

I remember the girls were close to 11 and Patrick was in diapers when they came down for Sunday dinner. Both their parents were working so they had brought the diaper bag and a couple sets of clothes for Patrick.

They were playing cards and watching TV when Ashley remarked, "Boy does he stink," holding her nose and pointing to Patrick. I offered to change him but Andrea was insistent, "I do it all the time, Grandma," and she proceeded to put the vinyl cloth down and get the diaper out. Patrick was a wiggle worm and Andrea clearly stated: "Little help here Ashley," and Ashley pinned his arms up over this head and as they touched the carpet, she said "Touchdown," which made him laugh, and me too!

The twins were in the band at school, and also several plays where instrumental music was called for. Since they were in the pit a lot waiting their turn to play on cue, they began playing cards, and since they were babysitting Patrick, they drug him along. Eventually he was pressed into playing Euchre when he was only 8 years old. He was good too!

After our son John was discharged from the Marines, he showed interest in police work also. He applied for and was accepted by Worthington Police Department, a nearby suburb of Columbus. He actually went through the Columbus Training Classes and graduated November 1, 1996.

This is taken from his graduation program, the Ninety fourth Recruit Class.

The Columbus Police Training Academy strives to develop skills, knowledge and attitudes necessary for the competent patrol officer. Its curriculum includes courses in Laws of Arrest, Search and Seizure, Police Courtesy and Discipline, Departmental Rules and Regulations, Applied Behavioral Operations, Vehicle Operations, First Aid and CPR, Accident Investigation and Traffic Enforcement, Civil Disorder Control, Police Weapons, Communications, Physical Training, Military Drill and Cultural Sensitivity.

    Total Hours in Academy Training ...............984
    Total hours in Field Training .......................360
    Total hours in Training ............................. 1344

    . . . . in 26 weeks.

# Chapter 47

About this time, my mother began to have issues with her knees, hip, and later her shoulder. She stayed in her home as long as she could, and then realized she needed to be somewhere she could get 24 hour care. After her hip operation, it popped out 7 times, and talk about pain! She went to a nursing home, the first of 7! After her knee operation she was in bed with those dreaded "TED" hose on, and when I walked in one day she was practically in tears.

"Mary get these off me," she pleaded.

I went to the nursing station and asked for a pair of scissors.

"What do you need scissors for?" was the comeback, "I can't just give them to you!"

As she turned her back and the scissors were left in plain view, I picked them up and returned to Mom where I proceeded to cut the stocking from toe to hip.

There, running along the inside of her leg, was a thin red line.

"I'll be right back, Mom" and I went to the nursing desk once more and asked them to call an ambulance; I was taking my mother to Riverside Hospital.

A nurse came in to see why Mom needed an ambulance and I showed her the red line. She explained that the house doctor would have to authorize this move . . . and he wouldn't be back here until Monday (this was Saturday).

"This is obviously an infection and I am not waiting until Monday. Get an ambulance or I will."

They stated that they could not hold a bed for Mom unless we paid for it and I strongly stated, "She isn't coming back here."

After she was started on antibiotics at the hospital she improved, and I once again began looking at places for her.

Actually there were two more places we tried. One was a private home in a rather expensive area and the lady who ran it was probably my age, and only had three ladies she cared for. It was nice, Mom had a private room and the food was home cooked and very good, but we felt it was too confining. Mom spent most all her time by herself since the other residents were either deaf or senile. Mom was neither.

Another time we moved Mom to "Arlington Court" and I was quick to notice the deficiencies of this place. One day I went in to see her and she was preoccupied with squeezing her finger.

"What's wrong, Mom?" I inquired.

"Oh, they come in every day and stick my finger' and to the nurse's station I went.

"Why are you sticking my mother's finger every day?"

"Well, is she a diabetic?" the nurse replied.

"No! She never has been . . ." and the nurse pulled a chart and remarked, "Oh, that was for the patient in bed 2 that passed away a few days ago. They just mistakenly thought it was your mom."

We moved her to another, and more expensive, place, The Convalarium. One day I was visiting her and she told me that she was uncomfortable on the commode, the extender was loose, and she was afraid she would fall. (An extender is a plastic molded piece that allows a patient to sit higher on the commode.)

I called the aide and asked that another extender be placed on the commode, as she was afraid she would fall off of it.

"Oh, sure, I'll get one, there are different types and I'll see to it . . . ." and off he went.

Sunday, I came to see Mom about noon. There she was sitting up in bed, her breakfast tray pushed up almost pinning her in bed and she had her leg propped up with pillows and an ice bag.

"What happened?" I said.

"I fell off of that extender. I tried to steady myself on it but it just tipped me between the wall and the commode."

I was furious! This is not how elderly people are taken care of. No use trying to talk to the aide or the nurse. I asked that Mom be taken to Riverside for x-rays. (This is when I think she tore her rotator cuff.)

Again, I would not take her back so we checked out, and at Riverside it showed she had a broken knee cap. Not much can be done for a knee cap, and I was reassured it would heal itself. Again, we were looking for a nursing home, and I checked out one close to my home. They had a bed, and Mom moved in. It was not Catholic, but they seemed kind and the place was clean.

One day I went over to see Mom and she had her rosary around her neck.

"Why do you have your rosary around your neck," I smiled curiously.

"Oh, that aide did that. I told her I wanted to wear some beads, and just look what she put on me"

I had to chuckle. This home was not Catholic, and she did miss going to Mass. She did some readings for the multi-faith services they had once a week.

She liked it there, played bingo and even euchre. But then, sometimes she would call me at 7:00 PM saying she did not get any dinner. I couldn't get there fast enough but did stop at a fast food place for a fish sandwich for her. I approached the Director of Nursing who assured me she would take care of it. Well, I had just had it! It happened again, once she was left in bed until afternoon, "short staff and a mix-up in assignments" was no longer acceptable.

Usually when one leaves a religious community such as I had, they sever all communication. I prayed and prayed, and told Mom to pray. I was going to St. Raphael's a Carmelite home, to see if they had any beds.

My sister-in-law, Peggy, went with me the next day. We met with the Social Worker who was very kind but very skeptical if they had a bed.

About that time, out of the corner of my eye, I saw a nun in a very familiar brown habit. As she passed the door, I wanted to follow her. As it was, she backed up, came in and we embraced. To this day, I will never forget the *"I'm Home"* feeling I had. She was a sister a year ahead of me in the Novitiate, Sr. Teresa Kathleen.

After a few "catch up's, how are you, family, etc," she asked what we needed. I told her my plight but unfortunately there were no rooms. She spoke to the Social Worker and they perused some room assignments.

"I think she would like rooming with Althea, Let's go look at the room". I was walking on clouds and we took the elevator to the second floor. I gave my sister a "thumbs up," and Sister Kathleen showed us "the room!" Althea, it turned out, slept on a mattress on the floor for her safety, as she had had several falls. This seemed to work for her. There now was room for a bed and Mom could move in ASAP. We even visited the chapel and said a prayer, then hugged Sr. Kathleen again.

I spoke to the Administration at Whetstone Center and told them mom was moving. My brothers, at this point, couldn't believe I wanted to move her again.

"She is going to be taken care of properly and this will be the final move, I promise. In my heart I knew this would be the "little bit of heaven" for Mom, and they had Mass every day. I was ecstatic.

I had told the nurses at Whetstone that I would be there at 11:00 to pick Mom up. My sister, Lois, came down from Toledo and Mom could ride in the car across town to Grandview.

We arrived at Whetstone at the appointed time. We walked into Mom's room, and she was still in bed. She had not had any breakfast and she was lying in a soaked bed since she could not get up to the toilet by herself.

A nurse's aide saw us and I couldn't hold it in any longer. Tears rolled down my face, as I retrieved a basin and soapy water. Lois packed her things while I bathed Mom and changed her clothes. A nurse did appear and I was very rude, "Thanks for having her ready. She did not even have breakfast. This is a fine farewell."

"I'm sorry, let me get a tray for her . . ." and she left. It was a good thing; I've never lost my temper in front of my mother, but she could see how exasperated I was. I will say, though in defense of this establishment, the aide did bring her a tray . . . . complete with cold coffee, eggs that were jelled in grease, and a biscuit you could have used for a hockey puck. How can you show such indifference to the elderly? What kind of care would mom get, if I had not come . . . again at the pre-arranged time. Of all days!!

# Chapter 48

St. Raphael's was a beautiful stone, two story structure, and at one time President George Bush, Sr., lived in the far northern part as a child. An addition made it quite the estate and eye-catching for anyone traveling by. There were rose bushes, trellises, and cherub angels decorating the entrance. A Kelly green canvas canopy led to the front door. Once inside, marble floors, gorgeous paintings, and ornate furniture adorned the spacious reception area.

The receptionist was a nun, a Franciscan, who greeted us warmly. I found out later she lived across the street at Our Lady of Victory, but enjoyed doing the switchboard and helping out wherever she was needed. She summoned two aides to help bring Mom's things in, and showed us to the room. Althea was sleeping, curled up in a ball like a little kitten.

The aide brought mom a snack since she had missed lunch. "She calls this a snack?" Mom replied, looking at a tuna sandwich, chips, pickle, jello cup, and a tea bag complete with little carafe of hot water.

Mom loved it from the very first day. I was so happy as were my brothers and sister. There were activities every day, and someone to push her wheelchair to the dining room. There were seminarians who came and visited with the residents, rosary said and Mass every day. I knew Sr. Michele from the Novitiate, she was in the "All Saints" category who was in charge of activities. She would visit with residents, carrying her guitar and sing everything from "Happy Birthday" to "The Rose of Tralee," a favorite Irish ballad.

There were porches on each floor at the end of the halls for visiting. Again, nice comfortable wicker chairs with pillows, and the sun would pour through the slatted window coverings. Everything was clean, polished, and scrubbed and you never knew when Sr. Kathleen would stop by.

One Sunday, my brother, Tom, was taking our mom out to his home for lunch. As he pushed Mom's wheelchair through the foyer, Sr. Kathleen eyed him from behind receptionist area.

"Hold on, sir. Mrs. O'Neil needs a sweater if she is going out."

"Oh she will be fine. My car is warm and . . ."

"I know, but I prefer she have a sweater on".

Tom rolled his eyes skyward and said, "OK" and Sister Kathleen had already called the floor for someone to bring her sweater post haste.

Another time, we still laugh at this. My brother, Dave and sister-in-law, Peggy, were visiting and I was gathering up Mom's laundry from the closet when I saw something in the back of the closet.

"Dave, what is that? It looks like a mouse" and he bent low to see into the dark cavernous closet.

We didn't have a flashlight to see, so he struck a match to get a better view.

"No," he said as he pulled out one of Mom's hairnets!! Whew, we were relieved it was only that.

About the same time, I was putting the laundry in the hall outside the door so I wouldn't forget it, when I heard Sr. Rose's voice.

"I can't find anything down here, guess we better call the fire department . . ."

"Sister Rose, No! My brother just struck a match . . . ."

"He WHAT?" I never heard her speak above a whisper until then.

We explained the best we could but she never cracked a smile. She was watching out for her residents.

A sister, who was stationed at St. Rita's before I entered, was stationed and died in West Palm Beach, Florida. She had been at St. Rita's and we became close friends over the years. I wanted to fly down for the funeral and was talking to Sr. Kathleen about my plans.

"Mary, don't spend the money. Just have a Mass said for her here; she would understand . . . ." she said.

I really wanted to go and even called to see if seats were available and prices. Something kept me from completing my plans, and I took Sr. Kathleen's advice.

When the horrible events of 911 took place, I shuddered, "I would have been on a plane heading south at that very time." It gave me more than goose bumps as on the following days we watched on television the horrible devastation that took place.

There was a "call out" for all police to watch over pertinent places in our city including the airport, Battelle Memorial Institute, the State Capitol, Ohio State University, etc. It seemed the world had stopped and people were swarming to churches to pray. There was nothing on television but coverage of the Twin Towers, New York City, the Pentagon, and plane crash in Pennsylvania, all the result of terrorism. How would America cope with all of this?

President George Bush II, choked up as he spoke of the devastation that changed the way our sense of security was threatened. America had suffered and to this day, everyone recalls where they were when the news interrupted television shows or they heard news alerts on radio. Employers sent men and women home to be with their families, and heightened alert took place as all airplanes were grounded.

Life seemed to return to normal, however the scars of the past would remain in our hearts, forever. Mom was happy at St. Raphael's and we had many special times with her. She was born at home on March 3, 1909 in Fleming, Ohio (near Marietta). When she turned 90 we had reserved the shelter house at Whetstone Park which was enclosed and had, of all things, an indoor fireplace. We had the party on February 27, 1999, and Mom was delighted to get a visit and card from her Pastor, Father Jim, from St. James the Less, her former parish. She also got a postcard from President Bill Clinton (and Hillary Clinton signed it too). She received over 50 cards, and some of her relatives from Marietta, Ohio came to help her celebrate her 90th birthday. Everyone had a good time!

Mom enjoyed the day, and when we took her back to St. Raphael's she insisted on taking a piece of cake to Althea, whom she was calling "Grandma" by now. As my brother Dave would say, "Mom, you are older than her!"

Father Dimond was my father-in-law's brother, my husband John's uncle. We noticed that he was not as sharp as he had been, and he was moved to Mohun Hall at Ohio Dominican University. They had a whole building dedicated to the religious nuns and priests and he seemed to fit right it.

He had married John and me, baptized both of our children, gave them their First Communion, was present when Cathy married Doug, and concelebrated the Mass for John when he married Vickie. He gave my father the last rites and performed the funerals for my dad and our daughter, Margaret. He performed the funeral service for my husband John and Janet's mother, Catherine, at Immaculate Heart of

Mary Church in Mercer, Pennsylvania, in 1964. He also presided at the gravesite service for Grandmother. He took ill and was rushed to Mt. Carmel East where he died, April 29, 2003. We miss Him as did many of the parishioners where he served.

THE REVEREND FATHER
ARTHUR J. DIMOND

Born: July 12, 1919
Ordained: May 26, 1951
Died: April 29, 2003

# Chapter 49

Mom's next "big" birthday was held at St. Raphael's in the Activity Room, she was 94, and it was mainly just family. It was obvious that she was beginning to fail and didn't get out of her wheelchair much. She would still play Bingo and proudly show off "her dime winnings."

I found this poem written in my mother's own handwriting. I doubt she was the author and wondered how it surfaced as I began writing this book.

### I LOVE TO LIVE

Today, Dear Lord, I'm 80 and there is so much I haven't done,
I hope Dear Lord, you'll let me live until I'm 81.
But then, if I haven't finished all I want to do, would you please let me stay awhile until I'm 82.
So many places I want to go, so very much to see, Do you think that you could manage to make it 83?
The world is changing very fast, there is so much in store, I'd like it very much to live until I'm 84.

And, if by then, I'm still alive, I'd like to stay 'til 85.
More planes will be up in the air, so I'd really like to stick and see what happens to the world when I turn 86.
I know dear Lord, it's much to ask (and it must be nice in Heaven), but I'd really like to stay until I'm 87.

I know by then I won't be fast and sometimes I will be late, but it would be so pleasant to be around at 88.

I will have seen so many things, and had a wonderful time, so I'm sure I would be willing to leave at the age of 89 . . . MAYBE just one more thing, I'd like to say, Dear Lord (I thank you kindly) but if it's OK with you, I'd love to live past 90.

Again, I don't know the author, but it is plain to see it is in my mother's handwriting but no date on it.

Sometimes we would get chicken, mashed potatoes, etc., and take it to share with Mom at St. Raphael's. We would set up a couple of tables on the indoor porch on the second floor. She would always want an update on the grandchildren and where everyone was working, etc.

One particular Sunday she didn't have much to say, in fact she could drop off to sleep in a second. We took that as a cue.

"I want to go home" she said softly. We weren't sure what she meant, so I leaned closer and asked her, "Where is home?"

No answer. So I asked, 'do you want to go to your room and lie down" to which she nodded yes. We wheeled her back down the hall and I got her in bed. I was still puzzled as to what she meant, so I asked again.

"Mom, where is home?" . . . and I waited. My brother Dave and sister-in-law were hovering near the door waiting to hear her answer.

I leaned closer, to hear . . .

"In my Father's house are many mansions, if it were not so . . . ." and she drifted off. We kissed her goodbye and she looked quite peaceful.

It was a busy week, getting ready for Thanksgiving, grocery shopping, etc. I was up late getting things prepared for our turkey day! It was just a little after 5 AM when the phone rang. I bounded out of bed; I knew no one would call me at this ridiculous hour unless it was an emergency.

"Mary, this is the nurse at St. Raphael's; I'm sorry to tell you, Mrs. O'Neil passed away . . . ."

"I'll be right there!" and while I dressed quickly I called Dave.

I drove at breakneck speeds since there was hardly any traffic at that hour. Speeding is not something police officers do unless they are in a car with lights and siren, but I had to get there.

Dave got there shortly after me. Mom looked so peaceful as they had cleaned her up and she had her hair combed nicely. We stayed until the men from the funeral home came, and Dave watched carefully as they rolled her into the ambulance.

We decided who was going to call who, and since it was Thanksgiving we would visit St. James rectory later. Funeral arrangements would be firmed up with Egan Ryan also later.

# Chapter 50

Her favorite poem was read at the service:

### The Divine Weaver

My life is but a weaving
Between my Lord and me
I cannot choose the colors
He works steadily.

Often He weaves sorrow
And I in foolish pride
Forget that He sees the upper
And I the lower side.

Not till the loom is silent
And the bobbins cease to fly
Shall God unroll the canvas
And explained the reason why.

The dark threads are as needful
In the Weaver's skillful hand
As the threads of gold and silver
In the pattern He has planned.

I love this poem by Helen Steiner Rice:

## WHEN I MUST LEAVE YOU

When I must leave you, for a little while,
Please do not grieve and shed wild tears
And hug your sorrow to you through the years,
But start out bravely with a gallant smile;
And for My sake and in My name,
Live on and do all the things the same,
Feed not your loneliness on empty days,
But fill each waking hour in useful ways.

Reach out your hand in comfort and in cheer
And I in turn will comfort you and hold you near;
And never, never be afraid to die,
For I'm waiting for you in the sky.

My brother and I went to Egan Ryan Mortuary and Jim let me pick out the casket which was white with pink roses! I was quite happy with my choice.

A rose is a special "sign" that means your prayers have been answered, or something you have been praying for will come true, or a number of other things. One time, when John was out of work, and had been applying for different jobs, I received a rose "out of the blue" from someone, and I nearly fainted. When I saw John later, I gleefully stated "You got the job!" He was perplexed and shrugged his shoulders saying, "We will wait and see." He got the job!

Statues of St. Theresa show her with roses, and many are devoted to her. Many prayers are answered, and the rose has become a symbol of love. I have received roses, (not from my husband because I know I would get a bill eventually,) in the way of artificial flowers, stationery, handkerchiefs, poems, bookmarks, a vase, etc.

# Chapter 51

Something that John and I have been doing for some 20 years now and enjoy very much is a monthly birthday party for the retired Dominican Sisters at Ohio Dominican University (formerly Saint Mary's of the Springs). The first Monday of every month we cross town to join in singing songs and serving cake to the most beautiful white-haired ladies you have ever met. Some still wear the habit, some are in wheelchairs or walk with walkers, some have dementia, but everyone enjoys the evening. The sisters having a birthday that month are given a long stemmed red rose and John takes their picture. The following month we will present their framed photo and their smiles are all we need in recompense.

Something I will never forget, nor will Janet, happened as we traveled to New York for a reunion of Carmelites who have left the community. This was such a warm and loving thing, to invite us back to Avila for a reunion with our "sisters."

This particular trip, Janet drove. She is a very good driver (see Janet, I did put it in here). I had wanted to stop and see Mother Gabriel, now in residence at St. Patrick's Home. She was the Vocation Director at Avila and we had communicated with her long before we entered. As Janet drove the streets of New York, it became darker and busier. We saw a rat cross the street near Central Park and Janet missed hitting it. (See, Janet, we could have cleaned up the city while looking for Van Cortland Park South.)

We stopped to ask directions. Some ignored us and some were helpful, but we still were having problems finding our way. Finally I said to Janet, "Let's just get a room and we probably could find it better in the daylight" . . . . and she agreed.

She suddenly and abruptly, turned into a drive and I said, "What is this?"

"Says Motel up on top of the building" so we got out, locked the car and went inside.

I thought it was rather barren but hey, this is New York.

I approached the desk, credit card in hand.

"We would like a room with two beds," I said.

"Uhmmm, you don't want to stay here . . ." the man behind the counter and plexi-glass remarked.

"Yeah, we do. She's been driving for 8 hours and . . . ." but I was interrupted again.

"No, sorry we don't take credit cards," he noticed the card in my hand.

"Janet, how much cash do you have?" I inquired.

As Janet moved up to my side, she noted what was on the desk top: "$100 . . . . one hour."

"Mary, let's go" and we turned and left. Never had I been exposed to such low class. Outside, Janet laughed and my naiveté showed.

# Chapter 52

Why is it that I find this next "chapter" of my life so hard to put in words? Why is my heart so heavy and tears cloud my eyes? What can I say? How do I say it?

I came in the door from work one evening and my husband met me in the kitchen.

"What are all those cars doing out front?" I began.

"Mary, listen to me. John has died; . . . . he took his own life," he sobbed.

I felt the kitchen spinning, my legs weak and John holding me ever so tight.

"What? How?" I begged. I was aware another police officer friend was with us, Dave Bowers, and later on I saw several more in the other room, homicide detectives. Being a police officer, I thought he was shot by a burglar, hit by a car, a random shooting . . . all kinds of things ran through my mind.

"John took his own life!" he finally admitted.

"NO, NO! Not my baby!" and John led me to the front room to sit. It was too much to sort out. "Why," I kept asking myself. John brought me hot tea and I thought the lump in my throat would prevent me from swallowing it.

Our John was always the "fun guy". One time I ordered chicken for the family, and his friend from the Marine Corps was here, so they offered to go and get it. When they approached the counter and gave the order, 36 pieces of chicken, fries, cole slaw, etc., and handed the girl a credit card, she asked, "Is this for here or to go?" They both looked at each other, shrugged their shoulders and said, "For here." Then when they got the order they proceeded to a nearby table and began going through the bags. The staff and counter girl could hardly believe their eyes. They finally got up, picked up the bags and left.

John was the fun guy the children loved to be around. He bought me a trampoline for Mother's Day, for the kids obviously, and he was the biggest clown on it.

Family and friends began to filter in and offer their condolences. Thinking of this day, February 16th, I remembered it was my sister-in-law, Peggy's, birthday. Oh, how awful I felt.

It seems that my nephew, Kevin, was working crime scene and they were at their desk when the call went out.

"Possible suicide at 1212 Northridge Street, decedent is a Worthington officer...."

"Let's go Kevin," his partner said.

"I can't go! I have to call my Dad. He is my cousin!" With that he called his Dad in Toledo and from there the word spread. At first, dispatch call, those privy to the radio channel, thought it was my *husband,* John.

A lieutenant from Worthington said that John had been very depressed over his divorce, and he had been there at his house hours before. He offered to take the guns out of the house, but John assured him he was fine.

The dreaded time came for calling hours. John stood by me as friends and associates of his came to pay their respects. We never sat down for two hours as people kept coming. John was dressed in his blue uniform and his hat perched in the casket with him. He had several medals on his uniform and it just was a nightmare seeing him, so still.

His funeral was quite large with officers from various departments showing up with their cruisers and leading us to the gravesite, Kingswood, where he would have a military burial. The cars and cruisers were too many to count. One sergeant from Worthington said people were calling City Hall to find out who died!

A woman approached us, crying and wringing a handkerchief. "I want to tell you how wonderful your son was to us. One evening we called the police station because our daughter had locked herself in her bedroom and was threatening to take her life...."

"Officer Dimond, your son, responded."

He had heard the dispatch, "I'm on my way," ... picked up his keys and headed to the address showing on the dispatcher's screen. John had lock pick instruments and was very proficient at it.

"When he knocked on the door, we invited him in and showed him to Megan's room. He worked quickly and found Megan had taken some pills; I didn't even know where she got them." she said.

"John took charge. He helped Megan stand up and had her follow him out the door. He said he would be back. We had no idea where they were going. She was stumbling, quietly crying, and could hardly keep up with his pace." She softly cried a little before continuing.

"They returned some two hours later. Megan was smiling and I could tell she felt better. They had walked, walked, walked, and walked some more. Lord only knows how many blocks they walked, around and around as he talked to her."

"Yes, John loved his job and helping people. How is Megan now?" I asked.

"She turned to her husband and standing behind him was Megan, tears streaming down her face, tissue in hand; she was inconsolable. She couldn't even speak. Her dad said that they had walked in the brisk night air, and ended up at Java Joe's where the black coffee John ordered for them which seemed to shock her back to reality."

We couldn't spend a lot of time with everyone due to the line streaking out the double doors of the funeral home. My feet were killing me from standing in heels for so long, but I was numb that so many friends came to pray with us, console us, and offer their services for anything we needed.

How his death impacted our whole family! The lieutenant walked up the aisle after the minister spoke, and retrieved John's hat, turned and took it to John's son, JJ, who was just ten at the time. It was a very touching moment.

The next day, a bagpiper stood and played "Amazing Grace" as many, many folks filed to John's place of rest. After the prayers were said, he played "TAPS," which always sends a chill through my body.

I found a "note" that my granddaughter wrote when she was 15. I found it in a tablet in my car after we had taken a trip.

> How dare you,
> You left us without warning.
> How dare you
> You left us shocked and sad.
> How dare you,
> You left us empty and miserable.
> How dare you,
> You left us mad at you

For even considering what you did.
How dare you,
You left us,
You died on your account
How dare you.

(in Andrea's own handwriting)

It has taken me three days to get through the most horrible days of our lives, John and mine. I have reopened the wounds and shed salty tears all over again. We have been able to share our experience with others who have had similar experiences, Janet for one in particular. John's sister, Janet (formerly Sr. John Catherine), had a beautiful daughter, Karen, who took her own life. They were inconsolable and again the question came up, "Why? She had a loving husband, a daughter, a good job, etc. so it was also a painful experience for our families.

What are the coincidences, brother and sister, John and Janet, both adopted, having a child who committed suicide? We have their memories but the hurt continues on and on.

Now I lay me down to sleep - John - 2/16/04

We are comforted by friends and family in our tragic loss. We weep in private that we will never see John on this earth, but know that in Heaven he has found his place.

John was a wonderful son! He was intelligent, humorous and loving. He was proud to be a Worthington Police officer and we heard many stories of him advising and helping teenagers while on duty.

As a young boy, John could ask some difficult questions, many we could not answer. He never gave us any trouble and his freshmen year he wanted to be a priest and went to PIME seminary in Newark. He finished high school at Watterson High School, he then joined the Marines Corps and served on Okinawa and the Marine base at Twenty Nine Palms, California. He married his first wife, Vicki, and together they had two children, a son, JJ and a daughter, Marissa, two beautiful children.

John loved to put on roofs (he did ours), do electrical jobs and wood working projects, was a locksmith (picked locks for the police department), loved movies, DVD's, going on cruises and scuba diving, playing with the children, and more.

John married Melissa, a dispatcher for the Worthington Police Department, along with their beloved golden retriever, Ranger, lived on Northridge Road. They had many good friends and loved entertaining at their house.

I guess we will never know why John took the stairway to Heaven, we miss him so much.

Thank you for your cards, prayers, food, hugs and sharing tears with us,

# Chapter 53

I had worked in medical offices and retired as I was having hip and knee problems, so no more police work. I had my right hip done first, then the knee. After the knee operation I felt a burning knot in my right calf, and sure enough was treated for a blood clot. Heparin shots and Coumadin (pills) got me through it, and a lot of prayers.

I have no doubt I had inherited by mother's bones and osteoporosis. She had had both knees, a hip, and rotator cuff operations. After a few months, I developed a spur on my left foot which was quite painful when I walked. I could scoot my foot along but bending it to walk was very painful. My podiatrist gave me prednisone injections, but soon it was quite apparent that surgery was called for. Since I had had the clot before, he sent me to a cardiologist for an intravenous "filter" placement. This filter would stop any formation of clots and insure that I would be fine.

I had the filter placement and the surgery the next day, March, 2012. Everything seemed fine, I had a cast on my leg from the knee down, and got around mainly in a wheelchair. I also had a knee scooter which I used at church and getting around on. One Sunday, at church, a little boy saw me and said to his mother, "Look, she brought her bike!"

To this very day, I do not know what made me ask John to take me to the hospital a month after the foot surgery. I did notice my legs felt heavy and maybe slight pressure in my lower abdomen. I just felt awful, not sick or running a temp, no, just a weird feeling.

It was midnight when we checked in at the emergency room, and thankfully they were not that busy.

"What brings you to the ER?" a resident doctor inquired.

"I think I may have a urinary tract infection . . ." and then some tests were run.

Minutes ticked by. John and I made small talk and were interrupted by the resident doctor.

"No, Mrs. Dimond, you don't have a UTI, but you do have a blood clot."

"No, I have a filter in place; Dr. Phillips put it in before I had the surgery . . ."

"Well, we are going to do some more tests including a Doppler, . . ."

"How many clots?" I asked.

"Well, as near as I can tell right now, many!" so I was whisked away for tests and more tests over the next five days. I was in the Cardiac Care Unit at Riverside Hospital then the step down unit.

John left the hospital and a phlebotomist was in to take blood, admissions came in to get more information, an IV was started, and I was exhausted. I know it was near 4:00 AM when someone came in and was standing next to my bed.

"What do you want?" I quickly retorted.

I turned my head, after noting the time, and saw my error; it was a priest.

"I'm sorry, . . ." I blubbered.

"Well they paged me to come over to give you the sacrament of the sick," and he did just that. I did not recognize him, and all I wanted to do now was sleep.

Next a certified nurse practitioner came in and attempted to cut the cast off my leg. At last the heavy cumbersome medical device was off, and I could breathe.

They gave me a clot busting drug (TP), and I looked like someone had taken a bat and beaten me with it. I looked horrible, and the days lingered on. I was moved to a rehabilitation center where I continued the Heparin and Coumadin. The day I was admitted there I heard one man say to another, "It looks like she tried to hang herself!". I stayed in my room for several days.

I will most likely be on Coumadin for the rest of my life, but that is just like insurance to prevent any more clots.

An interesting note here, I recently attended the funeral of a former parish priest, Fr. Smith, and I sat behind nearly 85 priests who attended. After Communion, I ended up on the end in the same pew with the priests as it was very crowded. I knew the priest next to me looked at me, probably wonders why I am sitting with the priests!

I looked at him about the same time, and he said to me, "I thought I recognized you. I gave you the sacrament of the sick . . . when was that?"

A brief conversation and then our attention was focused on the final moments of the Mass.

# Chapter 54

One of the jobs I enjoyed, (again a volunteer job!) was as a volunteer at Riverside Hospital. After training, I was assigned to the Orange Tower and I learned the hospital quite well. I've been rewarded tenfold just filling ice pitchers, feeding a patient, restocking shelves, etc. I've had to put this job on hold until after I have my left knee operation, which I am not looking forward to.

Also, I am a Eucharist Minister and take communion to the patients on a list prepared by the Chaplain. How blessed I feel to carry Jesus throughout the hospital and meet some very sick folks who are so appreciative of the little wafer I put on their tongue. A humbling job I look forward to doing.

Recently, I was making my Communion rounds and entered a room of a young man. "Would you like to receive Communion?" I asked. He paused the television and said, "Yeah, I'll take one!"

Another time, just as I was about to place Communion on the tongue of an elderly lady, she said, "Yes, you will have to come to my church sometime, the Church of Christ." I was a diplomat of my church and decided she needed a Protestant minister. I explained and left shortly thereafter.

# Chapter 55

It's been a long few months I hope never to repeat. John was directing traffic on September 1, 2012, after the first OSU football game. A car was coming towards him and John, using hand signals and blowing his whistle, was not able to divert this man's direction of travel. He took a quick step to the right and fell. He fell on his right shoulder and was able to complete the assignment, but by the time he came home I convinced him he needed to go to the ER.

It was not until November 30th that he was able to get the needed surgery, right rotator cuff, due to this being a Worker's Compensation claim.

John and I have had a wonderful life. He makes me laugh and I cry when he hurts.

It seems I have come full circle now, back with the Notre Dame sisters as I begin a year to become an Associate Member. Thanks, Mary Ellen, for allowing me the privilege of joining your group.

# Chapter 56

Peace be to all of you who read this, I hope you have enjoyed my life as much as I have.

### "Miss Me—But Let Me Go"

When I come to the end of the road
And the sun has set for me,
I want no rites in a gloom filled room,
Why cry for a soul set free?

Miss me a little—but not too long,
And not with head bowed low,
Remember the love that once was shared
Miss me—but let me go.

For this is a journey we must all take
And each must go alone.
It is all a part of the Master's Plan.
A step on the road home.

When you are lonely, and sick of heart
Go to friends you know.
And bury your sorrows in doing good deeds,
Miss me—but let me go.

Author Unknown

Edwards Brothers Malloy
Thorofare, NJ USA
June 5, 2013